Fifty-Eight Days
in the
CAJUNDOME
SHELTER

Fifty-Eight Days in the CAJUNDOME SHELTER

Ann B. Dobie

PELICAN PUBLISHING COMPANY

GRETNA 2008

The word "Pelican" and the depiction of a pelican are trademarks
of Pelican Publishing Company, Inc., and are registered in the
U.S. Patent and Trademark Office.

Library of Congress Cataloging-in-Publication Data

Dobie, Ann B.
  Fifty-eight days in the Cajundome shelter / Ann B. Dobie.
    p. cm.
  Includes index.
  ISBN 978-1-58980-579-8 (pbk. : alk. paper) 1. Hurricane
Katrina, 2005. 2. Hurricane Rita, 2005. 3. Hurricanes—
Louisiana—Lafayette. 4. Disaster relief—Louisiana—Lafayette.
5. Disaster victims—Louisiana—Lafayette. 6. Emergency man-
agement—Louisiana—Lafayette. 7. Family services—
Louisiana—Lafayette. 8. Lafayette (La.)—Social conditions. I.
Title.
  HV6362005.L8 D63 2008
  976.3'47064—dc22

                                        2008022069

Printed in the United States of America

Published by Pelican Publishing Company, Inc.
1000 Burmaster Street, Gretna, Louisiana 70053

For all those who suffered and for those who came to their aid in the aftermath of Hurricane Katrina and Hurricane Rita

Contents

Introduction 9

Part I   Coping with Crises
Chapter 1   The Fifty-Eight Days:
              An Overview 17
Chapter 2   The Story of a Family of Eight:
              Rescue, Relief, and Relocation . . . 25

Part II   The Rescue Phase
Chapter 3   Opening the Doors 31
Chapter 4   A Reporter's Notebook 55
Chapter 5   The Rescue Stories 61

Part III   The Relief Phase
Chapter 6   Making a Community 75
Chapter 7   Spaces and Places 95
Chapter 8   A Reporter's Notebook 99
Chapter 9   The Relief Stories 113

Part IV   The Relocation Phase
Chapter 10   The Diaspora 123
Chapter 11   A Reporter's Notebook 131
Chapter 12   The Relocation Stories 135

Part V   The Recovery Phase
Chapter 13 Acadiana Regroups 149
Chapter 14 A Reporter's Notebook 155

Index   157

Introduction

Those of us who have lived on the Gulf Coast for a few years know about hurricanes. We know the drill. First there is mention on the nightly weather forecast of a tropical depression miles away, and you hope that it will dissipate. A few days later it is renamed a tropical storm, and you rationalize that it is too far away somewhere in the Atlantic for it to be threatening to your home. Then as it crosses Cuba, slides around or over Florida, and moves into the Gulf, you pull out the hurricane chart you picked up from the television station and start marking the coordinates. Once it has been officially designated as a hurricane, you think about leaving, but still unsure about where landfall will be, you wait. You listen to the news. You mark the new coordinates. The storm begins to turn northward, and you check on the flashlight and radio batteries and make a grocery run to buy water along with canned tuna, soup, and chili. While it inches towards landfall, you watch with growing anxiety as the red ball on the television screen grows like an inflating balloon that covers the entire Gulf. You mark the new coordinates on the chart and see that the hurricane is taking aim on where you live. It is time to pack the freezer with bags of ice, put all the outdoor furniture away, and make sure the electric generator still works. You watch it begin to rain. The line of dots on the chart has met the land just where you are.

At the point of convergence, stage two of the experience begins. It is the essential story of the storm itself—the wind, the rain, the noise, falling trees, flooding, loss of power, darkness, and heat. Everyone has heard it and seen it. Television reporters include their viewers in the experience by going out in the tumult to demonstrate the strength of the wind—or their own foolishness. Their Eddie Bauer jackets whip around them as they show viewers the difficulty of standing up against the gale. They shield their eyes from the rain that lands like bullets on their faces. This is the hurricane itself, and at that point there is nothing more to be done.

In many ways, stage three of the hurricane experience, the aftermath, is the hardest. Certainly it is the longest. The process of preparation gives a person a sense of control over the gigantic force of nature bearing down, a sense of taking action that will diminish the threat of harm and destruction. In contrast, the experience of the storm itself is characterized by fear and helplessness. Instead of feeling in control, when the hurricane arrives, the storm victim knows that all one can do is wait. Watch, listen, wait. Neither of the first two phases of the hurricane experience demands the strength that the third requires. Although less reported by the press, and less noticed by the public, the efforts to recover are painful and enduring. The physical and emotional damage caused by the hurricane's crippling power can take years to repair. In some ways, the scars never disappear.

When Hurricane Katrina hit Louisiana and then

Mississippi on August 29, 2005, the destruction was vast. It swept away whole communities that are yet to begin rebuilding. A year later, jury trials in New Orleans had not resumed. Only three weeks and a few days after Katrina, Hurricane Rita ravaged the southwestern coastal parishes of Louisiana, leaving even more people without homes and functioning towns. Families that had lived in one place for generations were scattered across the country. It is not too much to say that every social institution and every person in the storm-damaged areas was touched and changed by Katrina and Rita.

For almost seven weeks, the staff of the Cajundome—a sports and entertainment arena in Lafayette, Louisiana—local volunteers, representatives from the Federal Emergency Management Agency, and the American Red Cross tried to cope with stage three, the aftermath of two major storms, Hurricane Katrina and Hurricane Rita. They struggled to create a livable community for people who had lost their homes, family members, and treasured personal possessions. More than 18,000 evacuees landed there, some of them having gone through horrendous experiences during and after the storms, many of them ill, and all of them needy. It was a gigantic effort at problem solving that went on for fifty-eight days. This is the story in all its complexity—its moments of transcendent human kindness and its incidents of malice, the selfless human gestures and the selfish, the noble and the base.

All names of evacuees in the stories found in this book are fictional, although their stories are real.

Fifty-Eight Days in the CAJUNDOME SHELTER

PART I

Coping with Crises

These are the times that try men's souls.
  —Thomas Paine, *The American Crisis*

CHAPTER 1

The Fifty-Eight Days:
An Overview

On the morning of Monday, August 29, 2005, the collective sigh of relief from Lafayette, Louisiana, was almost audible. Having made landfall between Grand Isle and the Mississippi River around 6:30 A.M., Hurricane Katrina was turning east, away from Vermilion Bay. With sympathy for those it was bound to hit and hurt, Lafayette gave thanks that it had dodged this one. Before the day was over, however, another kind of crisis had arrived. Greg Davis, executive director of the Cajundome, had been notified that his facility was a potential evacuation shelter. He could not know then what he and his staff, the American Red Cross, Federal Emergency Management Agency (FEMA), and local volunteers would be called upon to do and provide. He would have been staggered to learn that from August 28 to October 25, 2005, the Cajundome would house and feed evacuees from Hurricane Katrina, a category 4 storm that displaced more than one million people, and less than four weeks later it would be called to extend care to those fleeing Hurricane Rita—more than 18,000 people in all.

The events of Monday night only deepened the problems that Davis and his staff would have to confront. The levees in New Orleans failed, leaving the city in the grips of flooding, looting, and potential disease. With that scenario the Cajundome inevitably became a mega-shelter. Official notification arrived at ten on the morning of Tuesday, August 30, but the staff had little doubt that the space would be commandeered. Evacuees were scheduled to arrive after lunch, but in fact, they began coming within half an hour. With no preparation time, the staff had to move swiftly into new roles. They hastily set up registration procedures while operations director Phil Ashurst marked out floor space for people to occupy. Making quick reference to the checklist of building readiness needs that he had compiled from previous storm experiences, he began to call his events workers to set up and maintain the shelter. He checked emergency systems, paging systems, generators, and fuel. He locked down restricted areas. He wondered where he was going to find the provisions people would need: cots, mattresses, towels, and blankets. The pressure mounting, Sam Voisin, director of sales, would comment to Cajundome colleagues: "The events business is good preparation for running a shelter because both of them deal with fluid situations. They change minute by minute. To work in event management means being 'prepared for being unprepared.'" The rest of the staff was less sure. They were not trained for this duty. They just hoped their skill and experience in crowd control would be helpful.

The Acadiana area chapter of the American Red Cross arrived on Tuesday, along with John Francis Sheehan, Jr., community relations supervisor for FEMA. Local medical personnel and other volunteers began to show up, everyone trying to determine how to proceed. First things first, the doctors and nurses immediately started treating the arriving evacuees. Food appeared in just over an hour, and "Bubba crews," local groups of men who cooked, were engaged to provide the evening's meal.

By Wednesday a routine began to take hold. City-parish president Joey Durel assembled a task force of business people to consider what Lafayette's response to Katrina should be. Hurriedly they created committees to deal with every aspect of the storm's impact. The medical community set up a clinic in the Cajundome, and DeMarcus Thomas, a coach and educator, arrived to create recreational programs for children and adults. As it was the end of the month and Social Security checks were expected, Karen Jennings from the Social Security Administration met with Tony Credeur, director of the local American Red Cross chapter, to arrange for their distribution. Life seemed to be settling into a strange but predictable normalcy for the roughly 3,500 evacuees in the Cajundome.

The fledgling organization hastily put together in two days was not ready to deal with the new crisis that occurred early on Thursday, September 1. At one in the morning, more than fifty buses with around 2,700 evacuees pulled into the front drive of the Cajundome. All staff members, many of them on summer vacation, were hastily called back to process the new arrivals, swelling the operating staff from twenty-five or so to around 150 people. Almost 6,500 evacuees now occupied the building, and more remained in the parking lots.

Two days later another challenge presented itself, this time at 2:00 A.M., when an additional seventeen busloads of New Orleans evacuees arrived. They were exhausted, dirty, ill, and hungry, having been on buses since August 31 looking for a place that would take them in. Like other shelters, the Cajundome was full, but it gave them food, showers, and medical attention, even though they had to sit in the heat outside the building. By five that afternoon, buses from the Lafayette Parish Schools and the City of Lafayette had moved them to other shelters. They could not be registered to stay at the Cajundome, but they were welcomed and served there.

The quality of life at the mega-shelter improved considerably over the next couple of days. The Public Works Department of Lafayette Consolidated Government worked diligently to build twenty-four showers, two of them for handicapped use, by Monday, September 5. Around the same time director Greg Davis objected to the food being served by the Red Cross, claiming that it was neither nutritious nor tasty. Having made his point, he had the Cajundome take over all food service at that facility and the adjacent Convention Center. Hiring a chef and a nutritionist to attend to special dietary needs, the facility's food and beverage service, Artisan Catering, began to produce meals that looked and tasted better: scrambled eggs with grits, bacon, and biscuits for breakfast; shrimp Creole with rice and barbecued brisket with roasted potatoes for lunch and dinner. Morale began to rise. Local entertainment groups spontaneously appeared. The Conservatory of the Acadiana Symphony Orchestra presented "Music Time," a musical experience for the children, and bands came to give concerts, and choirs came to sing. The evacuees were even invited to attend a football game at nearby Cajun Field.

All might have gone smoothly from this point on except for Rita, another giant hurricane that, like Katrina, took aim at the Louisiana Gulf Coast. Because the Cajundome was not built to withstand hurricane-force winds, the Red Cross had agreed with Cajundome officials and the City of Lafayette years ago to use it only as a poststorm shelter, not as an evacuation center during a storm. Since the lantern area at the top of the building and the glass panels on its sides that could be dangerous in high winds were only part of the problem, on Thursday, September 22, the Katrina evacuees were evacuated again, moved this time from the Cajundome to the CenturyTel Center in Bossier City. By the time they began to return on the following Wednesday, the Convention Center had been opened as an additional shelter to care for Rita's victims, mostly residents of Vermilion, Cameron, and Calcasieu parishes. Nobody knew what to expect from the mix of urban, mostly African-Americans from New Orleans and the mostly rural whites from southwestern Louisiana. They were a diverse jumble of urban and rural, young and old, black and white. What they held in common was loss, need, and an unknown future.

By the beginning of October the number of residents at the Cajundome had begun to fall. The diaspora was in full force, with people who until then had never left their New Orleans neighborhoods getting on trains to places they could not locate on a map. By the middle of the month New Orleans mayor Ray Nagin had visited the Cajundome to make extraordinary promises of what FEMA would do and provide for those who returned to his city, and Calcasieu Parish had announced that everyone could return.

The numbers continued to drop. Security was reduced. Cleaning began at the Cajundome. On October 25, when fewer than 250 evacuees remained at the shelter, they were moved to the Comeaux Recreation Center. The crises were over.

For fifty-eight days the Cajundome had assumed a new identity. It had served as a hurricane mega-shelter in sharp contrast to its usual role as an events and entertainment facility owned by the University of Louisiana at Lafayette and Lafayette Consolidated Government. Opened in 1984 with an adjustable capacity of 4,500 to 13,500, the Cajundome usually presents an average of 140 events and ten to fifteen concerts a year. The facility had been designated as a shelter twice before Hurricane Katrina to provide short-term housing for people who were moving through, but it had never dealt with a catastrophe of this magnitude. Katrina, and then Rita, involved around 125 volunteers, eleven Master's Commission Groups, and ten organizations to help the displaced. Together they provided a total of 20,527 working hours. The shelter became a city in itself, offering the services provided by any community: food, shelter, medical care, mental-health counseling, postal service, laundry services, school, entertainment, security, transportation, even massages. It also became the site of human experiences that ranged from birth to death, through friendship, kindness, anxiety, and hope.

The success of the operation stemmed from the attitudes of all who were involved. The evacuees were treated with compassion and dignity, following the command of Captain Fowler of the Lafayette Police Department. As he instructed his officers: "You will assume everyone is a friend unless proved otherwise."

The evacuees responded in kind. James Proctor, a local volunteer, described the situation by saying, "Everyone was instinctively nice, gracious, and polite to each other. That includes the residents. They would hold doors for each other. There was a palpable feeling that we were all in this together. There was no time for conflict."

CHAPTER 2

The Story of a Family of Eight: Rescue, Relief, and Relocation

They are a family of eight now, although some of them had never met before they boarded the buses to escape Hurricane Rita. Jerome and Jared are identical twins, middle-aged, low-functioning, both in wheelchairs. Yvonne Senne is the mother of Tanya, who was just beginning to walk, and Serena, a quiet four year old. Yvonne's mother, Sherry, and her sister, Siona, belong to the family, too, and at the center is Donald Williams, Tanya and Serena's father, but in a sense a father to them all.

The group made their home in a corner of the Cajundome/Convention Center in Lafayette, where their beds lay side by side. Jared watched a television set placed in the small space next to his bed. Tanya moved from one to another, sitting in Yvonne's lap, holding onto Serena's fingers to try her baby steps. Donald Williams sat in the center telling the story of their journey, the physical one that wound its circuitous way from Lake Charles to Lafayette, and the other one, the inner journey that brought this group together as the family they had become.

Their story began with Rita's approach to the Louisiana coast. Watching the television updates through the night, Donald made a call to Yvonne to prepare her family to leave immediately. Taking what they could with them, they made their way to the Lake Charles Civic Center, where others were waiting to board buses that would take them to safety. Donald quickly moved to help those who were having difficulty making it on the bus. From the beginning he recognized the need for fast action. This trip was likely to take much longer than the usual trek to Jennings or Lafayette, and the night was sure to be a difficult one. Looking around the Civic Center, he spotted leftover food that they were sure to need. He gathered what he could, filling three vinyl trash bags with juice, water, Oreo cookies, doughnuts, and other snacks. He would later be glad he did.

Three of the buses were filled with special-needs patients—the elderly, handicapped, and diabetic. Rita was moving closer, and traffic had ground to a standstill. As Donald tells the story, he made his way to the front of the bus and advised the driver to follow his directions and to let the other two drivers know that they should follow in a caravan. Turning off the main highways, Donald led the three buses through "the 'hoods," the neighborhoods he knew would take them out of the city. Buses were not allowed there, but the three moved through them anyway. When they found themselves caught in traffic, Donald directed the driver to move to the middle lane and go as far as possible. The convoy moved forward.

The evacuees were anxious and fearful, uncertain as to where they were going or what would be waiting for them. Donald moved through the aisles of the bus using the skills he had acquired while working in a nursing home to quiet and soothe the fearful with words of comfort—along with water and the Oreo cookies. In the process he met Jerome and Jared, ... twins who would become part of his extended family.

At last the buses arrived at Beauregard High School in DeRidder, Louisiana, where the evacuees could spend the night in the gym. Donald instructed the twins to stay with him. He found them places to sleep in the bleachers, made sure Jerome took his medicine, watched out for their taped-up suitcase, and passed out more Oreo cookies. Hurricane Rita had found them. Its 130- to 140-miles-per-hour winds buffeted their building, but they were safe inside. As the night wore on, Donald took his flashlight and moved through the people, calming anxieties, serving those in wheelchairs. A woman known only as Mrs. Davis grew hysterical, and Donald helped her calm down. He used words when they could help; he spoke with his eyes when they could not. He stayed up for two days helping to make the evacuees as comfortable as possible.

But the situation resisted comfort. Almost one thousand people were lying on concrete floors in the large, un-air-conditioned room. There were no lights and no food. Sick people, babies, and others barely able to care for themselves sat and lay in the heat and darkness. Across the way the Red Cross was living in an air-conditioned building. Donald moved again, this time protesting the lack of basic needs. As a result, two fans appeared. Eventually even the air-conditioning was turned on.

What pushes people to move into positions of leadership? What makes them care enough not to be afraid to protest abuses and to serve as advocates for the helpless? Donald said he has always liked to work with "low-level people." He cared for his sick mother.

In a nursing home he even cared for his father, whom he had not seen in thirty-two years, for nine months before he realized who he was. Standing in "other people's footprints" made Donald see the world in a different way, and he will not forget the look of hopelessness on the faces of the people he left in DeRidder when he was transferred to the Cajundome. He left something of himself behind with them.

He has experienced many "footprints" since Hurricane Rita changed his life. Now he finds himself organizing outings on city buses for his new family, making sure the twins shave and shower, helping with Tanya and with Yvonne's diabetic mother. His efforts have not gone unnoticed. He has been congratulated and thanked by military personnel and Cajundome staff.

Does he plan to go back to Lake Charles? He's not sure where he will be in a few months, but he is sure that his new family will be with him.

PART II

The Rescue Phase

*Although the world is full of suffering, it is
full also of the overcoming of it.*
                            —Helen Keller

CHAPTER 3

Opening the Doors

When word was received on Monday, August 29, that the Cajundome was a potential shelter, operations director Phil Ashurst began to prepare the building. First employed as a stagehand at the Cajundome, by the time of Katrina's arrival sixteen years later, he was in charge of all technical services, engineering, electricians, production, facility maintenance, tear-down, and construction/renovation projects. He moves fast even on slow days, and on Monday he seemed to be moving double time. That night he began to apply his considerable experience and expertise to determining how many people could safely occupy the facility and how to fit them in. In addition, he checked all emergency systems and sent his calculations to the Office of Emergency Preparedness.

The biggest problem at that stage was getting staff on site quickly. Because Katrina occurred at the height of the vacation season, people were not at their usual posts and required time to get back to them. People who knew where to find things were too scarce, Ashurst said. Nobody missed the irony that the biggest event ever to happen at the Cajundome was going to occur when the staff was at its thinnest.

Using whoever could be found, Ashurst sent crews to clear storage areas in "tall storage," the table room, and some of the blue and green courtyards. Many large items were stored on the sidewalks surrounding the parking lots. All the ice floor covering was moved into the yellow courtyard to allow the center of tall storage to be used. Other equipment that could not be stored outside without protection from the weather was put into three twenty-foot offshore transport containers located in the grass north of the RV lot.

Kip Judice, security manager for the Cajundome and a full-time sheriff's deputy, ordinarily coordinates security for events at the Cajundome and the Convention Center. He is a quiet man who exudes strength, not at all the stereotypical southern sheriff. Ordinarily he is responsible for assessing each show to decide on the number of police officers that will be needed, which streets are to be blocked off, and other matters relative to maintaining a secure environment. After Katrina he had the same basic duties, but the numbers and disorder of those arriving complicated his job.

Having worked at the Cajundome when it was used as a shelter after other hurricanes, he had a mental plan of what needed to be done. The sheriff's office also had a model of security that had been devised for "volatile events" held at the Cajundome. It was not a perfect fit for this kind of situation, but it could be adapted for use. Access, Judice said, is always the key to a secure venue. "If you can control who and what comes into the building, you can control the situation." To monitor access, guards were stationed at every entrance and exit, making sure that nobody could go in except through the front entrance where there was a metal detector.

At the outset the process took place in four stages. The first stage involved getting people out of the buses and into the building as quickly and efficiently as possible. The second step was to set up a system for weapons detection. Security personnel searched bags by hand and used metal detectors as people entered. They found more than fifty guns, countless knives, and many straight razors. Sometimes they found other banned substances, such as alcohol and drugs. On the third day after the facility became a shelter, an officer searching through a bag found a can of Pringles potato chips. Upon opening it, he saw chips on top, but underneath he discovered a significant amount of drugs. It turned out to be the biggest drug arrest in the area for quite a while. Asked why he had searched through the can, he said, "It just didn't feel right." Security also found hundreds of illegal pills and crack cocaine.

The third phase of the process was to register each evacuee. This step inevitably slowed the process, and as the lines backed up, there were problems with people being pushed against the walls. To reduce the crowding, the security officers set up bike racks to form a buffer between the buses and the walls of the building. Finally, officers had to maintain an orderly flow into the arena so that people did not dispute space as they got settled.

Looking back, Judice recognized a need for more security personnel during these initial stages. In the crush of arrivals, people were sometimes stretched too thin, he said. The number of security people was increased as the Red Cross Safety and Security team carried out its customary duty to preserve an orderly environment in and around the shelter by working with Judice, local police, and the National Guard.

Hurricane Katrina quickly sent Sam Voisin, normally director of sales for the Cajundome, from sales to operations, which meant doing whatever needed to be done. Unsure of what to expect the first morning after the facility had become a shelter, he arrived as people were being admitted and asked Greg Davis what he should do. Davis requested he set up a shower system for three thousand people. Voisin found around two thousand towels reserved for artists who perform at the Cajundome, opened up the team showers, and started male and female lines. "I went from booking the Convention Center to handing out towels in a matter of hours," he said. His experience gave him insight into what the evacuees were feeling. "They came in whipped, covered with mud, sewage. They were not talking to each other. Hopelessness was written on their faces," he said. "The showers were a way to get the New Orleans experience off of them. They would go in with one mind set and come out with another. On coming out of the shower, one said, 'I smell like Lafayette now.'"

Bill Blanchet, assistant director of finance and operations, was at the Cajundome when the call came through that it was to be a shelter. At the time he was doing his normal routine—overseeing the accounting office, the food and beverage department, and the operations department. Initially he was not worried about what would be needed since he, along with others, expected the Red Cross to be there and take charge.

The Red Cross arrived about the same time as the evacuees, but never held a meeting with the Cajundome staff, leaving its members on their own to determine what should be done. Because there was no advance notice, there was not a prepared plan of how to handle the evacuees, and it quickly became apparent that the staff would have to work out a system to care for them as they came in. Blanchet cited the staff's experience in arena management as one reason they could effectively manage large numbers of people. At the outset it was simply a matter of finding space for people. Nevertheless, he pointed out, these were different needs from those the staff usually served. Instead of running concessions stands, they were providing meals and clothes—in short, they were serving very human needs.

Mark Tyrrell, manager of in-house food and beverage operations, was notified Tuesday morning that evacuees were coming from New Orleans that day. Having no idea how many people would arrive, he could do little planning. It was off season, and only a limited number of staff members were around to help. The kitchen was low on materials, too, but within seventy minutes of the arrival of the first evacuees, the kitchen had a meal ready.

Initially Tyrrell coordinated with "Bubba crews", police and service companies who cook for large local events, to cook on barbecue pits for two nights, and the Red Cross contracted with Baptist Men of Texas for early response. Many civic organizations showed up to cook for residents, volunteering their time, but a more permanent solution had to be established. After the first two days, the Cajundome was assigned the job of providing breakfast, and in response to objections that the Red Cross was not serving balanced meals, it took over lunch and dinner a couple days later. The Cajundome kitchen, under Tyrrell's direction, assumed responsibility for all food service at the Cajundome and the Convention Center. Nobody objected to that.

When the Cajundome went into operation as a shelter on Tuesday, August 30, there was no telephone service in or out of the building. Dave Prado, technical services director for the Cajundome, began looking into the problem by calling UCI Communications, the house telephone service provider. UCI informed him that New Vox Communications and its switch, which provides communications to the facility, were on Bourbon Street in New Orleans, which meant that service was inoperable.

Prado and Shanna Burton, a Bell South service manager stationed in Atlanta, worked together to get phone lines into the facility. UCI sent a technician to assist in getting communications back up by preparing the system for new analog lines from Bell South, which provided sixteen phone lines to the Cajundome in less than four hours, and Gene Benoit with AT&T arrived to begin locating and installing the lines to their demarcation points.

At the time the Cajundome became a shelter, Ashton Langlinais, president and CEO of WOW Technologies, had the responsibility of designing, installing, and maintaining all technology at the Cajundome. He moved immediately into providing the same services for the disaster-relief efforts. As he was already in the process of updating the Cajundome equipment, Langlinais was able to provide almost immediate computer capability. Because the fiber ring had been put in three years ago, he first made sure that the network was capable of handling all the local and national needs. This was the first time its capacity had been tested to this extent. The wait time for all agencies was less than an hour. The Red Cross technology teams arrived, but went on to other shelters because this one was already functioning.

During the first week of the shelter the staff had difficulty keeping up with all the necessary cleaning. Serious problems with trash handling and other housekeeping duties developed, and the "morning rush" added pressure to keep restroom and shower facilities cleaned as people woke up. On Sunday, September 4, Cajundome staff met with a representative from Our Lady of Lourdes Hospital to discuss sanitization of the facility, after which cleaning operations were substantially increased. Crews began to follow hospital cleaning procedures, including the use of antiviral chemicals. The cleaning staff was dramatically increased at this time to around seventy-five people, and two contracted crews were added.

Working alongside the Cajundome staff was the American Red Cross, though the respective duties of each organization were not always clearly defined. The ARC is chartered by Congress as a nonprofit agency, but it is not funded by the federal government. It was, in fact, the government's first nonfunded, mandated agency. Begun in 1881 by Clara Barton, a Civil War nurse, it is more than 125 years old. Since its inception it has opened and operated hundreds of shelters for people who have been displaced by disasters. It is important to note that the Red Cross does not accept the homeless in its shelters.

In its Participants' Workbook on Shelter Operations, the American Red Cross states its basic commitment: "To take care of eating and sleeping needs of the people affected by disaster on an interim basis while they are making other arrangements."

Shelter operations are described as a seven-step
process: preparedness, disaster occurs, preoccupancy
inspection, shelter opens, clients arrive, after disaster, and shelter closes.

Operating the Cajundome as a shelter proved to be
far less tidy and much less linear than this description
suggests. There was no time to prepare. Occupants
arrived before detailed inspections could take place.
Hurricane Rita interrupted the progress that had been
made and sent everyone back to the beginning. And,
finally, the magnitude of the impacted area, the
degree of destruction, and the number of evacuees
made it necessary for all caregivers to respond in creative, nontraditional ways that did not necessarily follow the guidelines set out in the manual. As a result,
the Cajundome mega-shelter was called many things,
ranging from "a highly unusual operation" to "the
Hilton of Red Cross shelters."

As the local Red Cross leader, Tony Credeur was
included in discussions regarding the use of the
Cajundome as a shelter in the meeting held at the
office of city-parish resident Joey Durel on August 30.
Because the local ARC agency is a first responder,
Credeur and his five full-time staff members became
responsible for seeing that the immediate needs of
evacuees—food and shelter—were met. National volunteers began arriving shortly thereafter.

Teresa Ellis and her husband, Tom, were the
national volunteers who served as the Red Cross
management team that worked in conjunction with
the Acadiana chapter of the ARC. Together they over-
saw the Cajundome and the seven outlying shelters in
the Acadiana area. Teresa, who was responsible for
the operating services at the Cajundome, had been

with the Red Cross for 15 years, but she had never worked with a disaster or shelter of this size. Her experience included organizing a local chapter in her hometown in 1990, then assuming responsibilities for disaster preparedness on the state level in Indiana.

Problems came in all shapes and sizes. In the early days of the shelter, communication between volunteers at the Cajundome and Red Cross headquarters in Baton Rouge was sporadic. Even when headquarters personnel were reached, support was minimal because the staff was thin. Some of the volunteers described the sketchy communication as fortuitous because it allowed those on site to do what they knew needed to be done without first getting approval.

A potentially serious problem involved the relationships among all the agencies working at the Cajundome. Initially their areas of work and decision making were neither clearly defined nor comfortable. Deciding which areas of responsibility belonged to the Red Cross and which came under the aegis of the Cajundome was particularly problematic for a while. On September 8, the *Lafayette Daily Advertiser* reported on a particularly sharp exchange in which Greg Davis publicly criticized the Red Cross for not distributing several thousand cots to people who were sleeping on the concrete floors of the Cajundome. The paper quoted him as saying, "I am angry about what has happened to these poor people. . . .We have failed them. It could have been avoided. That's what angers me." He cited as evidence the lack of bedding provided for the first arrivals, who were forced to sleep "on the concrete floor without cots, inflatable mattresses, or even blankets and pillows." The anger mounted when, as he reported, "we found a tractor trailer truck on our property that was parked behind the Convention Center two or more days that belonged to the Red Cross. We investigated and found they had five thousand cots. . . . We were able to secure those cots and aggressively distributed them to our guests."

Because of the ARC's policy of not giving out supplies unless all those in a shelter can have an equal share, the cots had been stored in a truck parked just outside the facility. Armed with that information, Davis took immediate action; he got the keys, unlocked the truck, unloaded the cots, and gave them out as far as they would go. Not everybody had to spend the night sleeping on concrete.

And Davis didn't stop there. Next he took on the food service. The *Daily Advertiser* reported that he authorized the purchase of two hundred thousand dollars worth of food "because we thought that evacuees who had spent three, four, five days on the top of a roof required more than a donut or a honey bun for breakfast, lunch meat on stale bread for lunch, and chili out of a can for dinner." The Red Cross public information officer, who was from Orange County, California, denied any knowledge of bad food or unused bedding.

FEMA is not a first responder, but it arrived early in Lafayette in the person of John Francis Sheehan, Jr., a FEMA community relations supervisor. When first responders, local and state officials, preparedness people, the National Guard, and the Red Cross are overwhelmed, FEMA is called in. According to Sheehan, FEMA works closely with the Red Cross, as it is a sister emergency-response agency.

The mission of FEMA is to come into a disaster to

organize and coordinate the many agencies that are involved with disaster relief. The federal response plan, which sets out who is responsible for what, has twenty-six signatories. It is FEMA's job to see that they work together to provide help to those who have been affected by the disaster. Although most FEMA workers at the Cajundome acknowledged that their organization has changed significantly since it was put under the direction of the Department of Homeland Security, they denied that the changes have significantly affected their work in this kind of crisis. The modifications, they said, are primarily at the upper levels where there is great concern with terrorism.

What FEMA people do varies with the stage of the disaster. Sometimes they are involved in preliminary damage assessment, but primarily they work as a recovery group. The earliest stages begin with a meeting between FEMA and the parish emergency manager to explain what FEMA can do. FEMA then asks to be taken to the most damaged part of the parish (or other site) to assess the nature and extent of the task.

Up to this point in the process FEMA looks for community leadership—mayor, parish president, sheriff—but then the attention turns to the "multipliers"—groups or organizations that have outlets that can serve to disseminate information throughout a community. An agency on aging, for example, has many senior-citizen centers that can be used as information distribution points. In the most severely damaged areas, FEMA representatives often go door to door—if they can—to reach people who were affected by the disaster and explain how to register, giving them the toll-free FEMA phone number and informing them that they may be eligible for help. Once the victims have filed, they can access their computer files at a Disaster Recovery Center.

After Katrina, Sheehan supervised up to six field specialists in the Cajundome and throughout the thirteen parishes in southwest Louisiana where people could get help with FEMA programs and applications. After August 30, Sheehan traveled through each parish each week to meet with his field teams and talked with them frequently by cell phone. Sometimes assistance was offered at community meetings, although, according to Sheehan, people are less honest in group settings than they are face to face. Meetings can also be inflammatory, whereas difficult situations are more easily defused with a personal discussion.

Tricia Schaefer, a Strike Force team leader and FEMA liaison with Lafayette Parish during Hurricane Rita, arrived September 1. She immediately began working with evacuees at the Cajundome to determine their needs. Next she set up a booth to provide information, scheduled buses to the Disaster Recovery Center for evacuees to check on their claims, and in general, tried to put out fires and cut through red tape.

Until all the FEMA representatives could arrive, employees of Parkerson Brinckerhoff, an engineering firm hired to inspect houses, were used to register people at the Cajundome. Since they could not do the housing inspections for which they were hired, FEMA gave them two days of training and deployed them to shelters across the area.

Schaefer was realistic about the shortcomings of FEMA. She admitted she would have liked to see the time it took to get housing shortened and in general been able to get help and money more quickly. She noted that personnel had been stretched because the need was so widespread. She herself had another job that was not guaranteed when she was called up by FEMA, a policy that diminishes the number of people who can afford to work for the agency in her capacity. She also would have liked to see a better relationship between FEMA and the Red Cross, but she praised the Cajundome staff and all the hospitality and assistance they gave her. For example, when speaking of the evacuation when Rita was approaching, she said, "The evacuation plan was awesome, and its execution was like a well-oiled machine. The staff was hard on themselves, wanting everything to be perfect. The plan should be written up and distributed. It should be a policy."

Sheehan, too, acknowledged that FEMA is not without problems. As he pointed out, in its haste to help, sometimes it hurts. For example, trying to get money to people quickly with a two thousand dollar check or electronic-funds transfer became problematic because some of the evacuees had so many addresses that they were hard to find. In addition, a letter explaining how to spend this money did not accompany electronic transfers. And sometimes the letters that were sent simply got lost. Consequently, some of the evacuees used the money inappropriately. Other problems were caused by FEMA's practice of starting programs and then closing them. When the status of the relief keeps changing, everyone is confused, including the workers.

FEMA representatives, who are known as community-relations specialists, stay in the community and often become friends with the people affected by disasters. Because they want to be part of the local environment, they go to area churches and public functions, present programs in schools with the students, and wear their shirts so they will be recognized. They see themselves as people of good will trying to comfort those who have been hurt, to assure them that everything will be all right, that the community will return to normal. Sheehan calls them missionaries. He is convinced of the importance of FEMA and is proud of what it does.

By all accounts the emergency medical treatment that was rendered in the first few days and weeks of the Cajundome shelter was heroic. Like other caregivers, the medical personnel had no preparation time. They had to move quickly because there was no agency on site to provide medical care at the beginning. The paperwork required by Health and Human Services to establish a clinic would have taken them two weeks. The American Red Cross, which is dedicated to providing food and shelter for people, offers little more in the way of medical care than first aid—including blood pressure checks and over-the-counter drugs—and referrals to hospitals. Local medical personnel with the help of doctors and nurses from all over the United States, France, and other countries moved in to fill the void. They arrived immediately—unasked and uninvited—mobilizing quickly to provide the care that was critical to the well-being of the arrivals. They came because they recognized human need. Within twenty-four hours they had an emergency clinic up and running.

Dr. Paul Azar, who had had military training in setting up MASH units, was in charge of organizing the medical care. Dr. Charles Wyatt of the Cardiovascular Institute of the Southwest and Dr. Andy Blaylock were also deeply involved. Under Dr. Azar's direction, doctors and nurses, like Cyd Begnaud, Jody Mittiga, and Stephanie Day, met the incoming buses on Tuesday, August 30, boarding them to assess the passengers' conditions before they were unloaded. Although the evacuees were dirty, smelly, and some of them ill, the medical caregivers knelt in the aisles to check them, not one of them turning away.

Because many of the evacuees were not leading healthful lives before they were forced to leave their homes and they had suffered through the unhealthy atmosphere of New Orleans after the storm as well as the trauma of losing so much, they needed immediate attention. After triage, those in dire need, such as patients who had not had dialysis for days, were immediately sent to hospitals for care. The rest were treated in the Cajundome's second-floor emergency clinic.

The most bothersome problems encountered in the clinic, according to the medical professionals who were there, were not medical ones. They were more often problems of red tape, bureaucratic delays, and conflicts with other agencies such as the Red Cross. Also, the location of the emergency clinic on the second level of the Cajundome was inappropriate, because it required patients to walk up stairs to reach it. After days of giving care, the medical team was served with legal papers saying that they would be sued because an individual with disabilities could not get up the stairs to get medical attention. The doctors and nurses had been going downstairs to help such cases, but the threatened law suit expedited the decision to shut down the emergency clinic and move it to University Medical Center on September 9. Later it moved to other medical facilities.

The clinic's staff of more than two hundred medical personnel treated more than 3,500 patients in the three weeks that it was open. They treated a wide variety of medical needs, including high blood pressure, depression, drug addiction, ear infections, eye infections, tuberculosis, heart attacks, pregnancy, and gallbladder, neurological, and diabetic problems. (Diabetics demanded much of the attention.) They dealt with bacterial infections and an outbreak of the Nora virus, known as the cruise-ship virus. In addition, patients were treated for bone fractures, cuts, and bruises. At least one evacuee suffered third-degree burns on his face caused by the heat in the attic of the home in which he survived the storm. Pregnant women nearing delivery were sent to University Medical Center. Tuberculosis patients were isolated. Methadone users were transferred to a methadone clinic, and mental-health cases were referred to appropriate specialists for treatment. There were no deaths and no epidemics.

Medicines were supplied by local doctors and drug providers. Lee Trahan, a drug representative, picked up medicines for the clinic from doctors' offices. Lafayette Parish Medical Society, through Dr. Ron Clark, also donated drugs. Eventually the doctors at the clinic got authority from the state of Louisiana to write prescriptions, and Walgreens offered to provide anything they requested. Until that time they refilled the medications they could understand, but at all times exercised caution about narcotics, enforcing a no-tolerance policy.

A number of faith-based organizations provided

exemplary service during the mega-shelter operation. One highly visible group was the Pastor's Resource Council (PRC), representatives of a network of five hundred to one thousand multidenominational like-minded pastors and churches across the state that seeks to address community needs and distribute relief. The PRC network was established by Gene Mills, who is now president of PRC Compassion, a charitable organization that is in a strategic alliance with the Pastor's Resource Council. Its stated mission is to coordinate national, state, and local faith- and community-based organizations to meet the physical, emotional, and spiritual needs of people impacted by Hurricane Katrina. That goal was addressed through five projects—providing temporary shelter, supplying food and water, furnishing heavy equipment, sending laborers to clear fallen trees and work in the shelters, and finding counselors for the emotional needs of those affected by Hurricane Katrina and its aftermath.

PRC's involvement with the Cajundome shelter began when Pastor Jacob Aranza walked into Greg Davis's office on Sunday afternoon, September 4 to ask, "What can we do for you? Can we have a service? Minister to people?" Davis's response was that while he had many people who wanted to minister, he needed people who would clean, sanitize, set up cots, and help with the logistics. Aranza replied that his people could do all that. By that afternoon he had brought someone in to serve as personal assistant to Davis, appointed a person to be in charge of cleaning with five full-time cleaning teams rotating every six to seven hours, and formed a full-time labor crew to sanitize and clean buses and cots. With a revolving group of young people, the work continued. Easily recognized by the bright orange T-shirts they wore, they could be seen each morning filing into the arena to collect laundry, clean the sleeping areas, and calm those who were afraid. In general, they quietly did what nobody else wanted to do.

During the operation of the shelter, PRC brought more than eight hundred volunteers to Lafayette at the same time that it expanded its areas of service. As the extent of Katrina's damage became known and after Rita struck, the breadth of its efforts broadened to include eighty shelters from Beaumont, Texas, to Biloxi, Mississippi, with more than thirty points of distribution, each as large as a K-Mart store. Around two thousand men and women with chain saws worked to clear trees and debris, and others delivered more than one thousand semi-truckloads of goods to areas of need. They pledged to continue their relief work for the next year and committed themselves to the rebuilding process that would follow over a five-year period. They made it known that they planned to stay at the Cajundome "until the last person leaves." All of their work is not for profit.

The way PRC organized and carried out laundry services at the mega-shelter is typical of the way the organization works. An explanation of that process can provide some insight into the group's commitment. On Monday nights, PRC volunteers would pass out bags in which Convention Center residents could deposit their personal laundry. On Tuesday mornings the PRC collected the bags for Single Source Supply to pick up. (A laundry that serves area hospitals, Single Source was known to have high standards. It provided its services to the Cajundome and Convention Center residents at cost, not for profit.)

When the bags of clean garments were returned that evening, the PRC volunteers would distribute them back to the families, who were identified by numbers on the bags, which had also been entered into a computer database. On Wednesdays, PRC performed the same service for the Cajundome residents. On Thursdays and Fridays, they took care of all the linens collected during the week. When a family moved out, its towels and linens were laundered and returned to the distribution center.

The word "compassion" that follows the PRC initials on the volunteers' orange shirts is the key to understanding its mission. Regardless of the duties and services the volunteers performed at the shelter, they always put the human side of their work before everything else. For example, in the sleeping/living areas they would go ahead of the cleaners to move items so that the floors could be swept. It was the job of the PRC volunteers to explain to the residents what was happening so that they did not feel threatened or bullied. They provided care on a very personal basis. As Mark Carter, site director for PRC, said, "You get to know some of the families on a personal basis. You build a relationship with them and learn what they've been through."

The Foundation for Hope is a faith-based, non-profit outreach program that provided welcome assistance in finding homes for the evacuees. Initiated by the Coast Hills Community Church in Aliso Vieho, California, the foundation works in coalition with churches and Christian ministries across the country to provide evacuated families with permanent and transitional housing that will give them a sense of normalcy, privacy, dignity, and comfort. After Katrina

and Rita, it offered families who were willing to relocate outside of Louisiana furnished houses or apart-
ments with food, rent, and utilities covered for ninety
days, assistance with job interviews, and help with
getting children enrolled in new schools. The intent
was to enable families to live together as they
returned to lives of independence. Funding and support for their efforts came from churches that were
invited to sponsor families and make donations that
would cover the cost of families' needs. The project
was highly successful at the Cajundome, and when
the capacity of those working there was exceeded by
the demands for the Foundation's services, the
agency formed a partnership with the Pastor's
Resource Council to increase the number of its workers and extend its network to five hundred churches
across the state. In all, the foundation worked on 150
cases, placing about forty-five families (approximately 180 people) and finding jobs for more.

Carrie Steegler, a team leader for the Pastor's
Resource Council at the Cajundome, went on to train
new volunteers in Baton Rouge through City Team, a
volunteer organization that continues to implement
the Foundation for Hope model. When the
Cajundome ended its shelter efforts, there had been
no decision about whether the Foundation would end
with the efforts to help victims of Katrina and Rita or
whether it would continue to serve those hurt by
other subsequent disasters.

From the time Katrina became a threat to the
Louisiana coast, Lafayette Consolidated Government
had a serious stake not only in what effect evacuation and relief efforts would have on the city and
parish, but as co-owner of the Cajundome, it also had

specific concerns about how the facility would be used. Consequently, well before Katrina struck, the Office of Homeland Security pulled Lafayette Consolidated Government into the prestorm planning, and city-parish president Joey Durel, along with other local officials, willingly agreed to do all they could to provide rescue and relief services to whatever areas were hit.

Durel also recognized the need to see that Lafayette's security and well-being were protected through what promised to be a time of disruption and strain. In the first twenty-four hours after Katrina's landfall, Durel assembled a task force of respected business people to consider what Lafayette's response to Katrina should be. Within forty-eight hours he called its first meeting to urge the members to be proactive about the immediate needs of the city as well as long-range concerns. His intent was to position the city to help people in the devastated areas, assist with the rebuilding efforts, and expand Lafayette's infrastructure so that present and future populations will be well served. The task force created committees to deal with every aspect of the community.

After the first hurricane struck, local government provided ancillary services from the fire department, sheriff's department, National Guard, city police, and the city marshal. When the Cajundome became a shelter, the Public Works Department, at Durel's direction, began building shower facilities for the evacuees. The city also provided taxi vouchers for evacuees to travel to doctors' appointments, hospitals, and pharmacies. With buses from private vendors added to the city buses, new routes made it possible for evacuees to get to FEMA services and other government offices. Reimbursement was to be provided by FEMA.

At the same time that Hurricane Rita reached Lafayette, Lafayette Consolidated Government received a phone call from Baton Rouge notifying officials that a check for more than $8 million was available from the Office of Emergency Preparedness. To expedite and protect delivery, chief administrative officer Dee Stanley requested a police escort to drive to Baton Rouge to get the check while Rita was in progress. Even the rain and winds did not delay receipt of the funding, $6.5 million of which was earmarked for the Cajundome. The usual practice is to pay expenses, document them, send the receipts to the federal government, and receive reimbursement, a process that sometimes takes years. The check from the OEP allowed the Cajundome to have a positive cash flow without waiting for reimbursement. Because it was issued between the two storms, problems developed about how to account for the Katrina evacuees as separate and apart from the Rita evacuees. Since there was no way to distinguish accurately between the two, FEMA finally decided to treat them as a single group.

Sometimes the city performed well despite mistakes and accidents. Most often it was miscommunication that led to wasted efforts among rescue and relief workers. For example, Durel was asked to provide five buses to pick up evacuees in Baton Rouge. He agreed to cover the four thousand dollars cost, but only two of the buses returned with people. On another occasion, three days after Katrina hit, the city received a call that five Blackhawk helicopters were being sent to Lafayette loaded with ill and injured patients. Local officials were asked to provide a decontamination team, twenty-two ambulances from Acadian Ambulance, as well as doctors and medics. The group assembled at the Lafayette airport and waited, but the Blackhawks did not arrive. Calls to Homeland Security revealed that they would land in thirty minutes, then in ten minutes. After waiting an hour and a half, the assembled medical group was notified that due to pilot fatigue and the patients' conditions, the flights had been canceled. A similar incident involved two trains that have come to be known as the "ghost trains." Set to arrive in Lafayette, they were to deliver six hundred people who would then be transferred to buses to go to Houston. A police presence was put in place, but the trains never appeared. Later on, a single train arrived with one-fourth the number of people expected.

Despite mix-ups, Lafayette played a major role in the rescue and relief efforts following both storms. According to Dee Stanley, the massive destruction caused by Katrina and Rita created a situation worse than those found after natural disasters in third-world countries because the entire infrastructure was destroyed in many places. Towns and parishes could not help themselves recover because the very agencies charged with implementing the recovery had been lost. The fire departments, police departments, and other support systems were gone, leaving the military as the only available authority. However, because lives have to go on, a minicity had to be established to remake what was lost. Lafayette, principally through the shelter that the Cajundome became, provided that temporary civic and social community that so many had lost.

CHAPTER 4

A Reporter's Notebook

Tuesday, August 30

Lafayette missed the initial bullet, Katrina itself. But news has just come through that it will be a major player in the second phase, the rescue and relief effort. What does that mean for our city? Nobody knows. Some people are prophesying doom, and others are preaching civic responsibility. I haven't been in this situation before and hardly know what to think. What should I be doing? What can I do that would help?

I guess everyone—except the doomsayers, who are sure that we will become another Superdome disaster scene—is asking these questions. Acadiana is a giving, generous place, and on balance I think it can be expected to serve and minister to whoever is coming. We will see.

Wednesday, August 31

It's hard to realize the scope of the devastation and loss, especially when life for those of us who are relatively untouched goes on as usual. Tops Woodwork came to my house today to measure for new kitchen counters, and at the same time people who have no possessions at all are arriving at the Cajundome. I'm concerned about granite kitchen surfaces when some people don't have clothes or critical medications? There's something wrong with that picture. The evacuees are just down the street from my house and a world away. How can I blend the two?

Thursday, September 1

I hear that people are volunteering to help at the Cajundome. Help how? I've never done this sort of thing, and I have no experience to offer. I drove by this afternoon, or at least got as close as I could. The grounds seemed to be awash in people, people walking, sitting, talking, smoking, staring off into space. I couldn't stop because the parking area was blocked off, but I drove as slowly as I could, trying to get a sense of what it's like inside.

It is reported that supplies are short, but that donations are being dropped off in huge quantities. I guess they need everything.

Friday, September 2

The Cajundome is said to be full of children. I am told that the entire space is so crowded they are forced to spend much of their day on the cots or in small enclosed spaces. The families don't want to leave their "places" because they fear losing the few items they still possess. And that means the children have to stay with them, too.

Realizing how traumatic all this must be for the displaced kids, the Grief Center has planned a Kids' Play Day at Girard Park. They've engaged a fairly large number of organizations, agencies, and individuals to be there to play with the children. It will be interesting to see how it goes. Will the children be afraid of the strangers there?

Saturday, September 3

It's happened again. At 2:00 A.M., seventeen bus-loads of New Orleans evacuees who have been on buses since August 31 arrived. The Cajundome is full now, and those who can't be registered are sitting all around the building.

One positive outcome of the Katrina disaster is my husband's closet. He has been moved to go through clothes he hasn't worn for years to find what he can give away. We took a huge stack of garments to Goodwill this morning and had to stand in line to hand them over. Many people seem to be doing the same thing. I haven't seen his closet this empty for years. I could swear some of those shirts dated back to high-school days. He swears they didn't, but I won't quibble as long as he gets rids of them, especially since someone else needs them.

Sunday, September 4

Apparently the Cajundome has people everywhere. Inside they are shoulder to shoulder; outside they mill about the parking lots and driveways, lean against the brick pillars, and sit on the sidewalks. They engulf everything. They make up a city of families and strangers, but not a community. A friend who is serving as a volunteer says that the families huddle together, afraid of losing sight of each other, afraid of losing the few possessions they have brought or been given. The strangers are suspicious of each other and jealous of their space. Occasionally someone spots a missing family member or a friend from another place, and for a moment the suspicions melt away in the face of recognition and trust.

To enter this instant city you must go through a

gauntlet of inspections: metal detectors, purse searches, identification presentations. The newspaper reports that at some shelters the Red Cross simply marks the back of evacuees' hands with a black *X*, and at others they give out wristbands to designate who is a registered resident. In the twenty-first century such methods seem medieval to me. How quickly we can be stripped of the trappings of the computer age and sent back to rudimentary methods of keeping track. Why isn't everyone's information entered into a database that could be crosschecked with other lists—lists of sex offenders, criminals, missing persons, for example?

Monday, September 5

At church yesterday the priest mentioned that the number of people living on the street in Lafayette is growing daily. He knows this because the mission our parish operates downtown is seeing a significant increase in people—almost all men—attending services and asking for help. These are the last people who are likely to receive assistance, since most of them will be turned away by the shelters because of alcohol or drug problems.

My priest says the homeless men need basic health and sanitation packets: soap, toothbrushes and paste, wash cloths, combs, razors, and more. All those friends from across the country who have asked how they can help are about to hear from me. I know my colleagues in the National Writing Project who have been sending messages of support from all over will come through to help these men.

Wednesday, September 7

I've written a letter to NWP friends from California to

Maine asking for help. I sent them an e-mail that said:

O.K., Writing Project Folks, this one should be right up your alley. You know all those little shampoo and lotion bottles that you have collected from all those hotel stays? We need them. The street people who have arrived here from New Orleans lack the most basic personal items, so we are putting together some "health kits," really just big baggies filled with soap, shampoo, and other items for hygiene. If you want to throw those bottles into a box or strong envelope and mail them to me, I will put them into the baggies myself. They will be distributed by a down-town mission to those who need them. We know the group is growing because the number of people who attend services there has doubled over this past week.

Thursday, September 8

If my National Writing Project teacher friends can be generous when it comes to homeless men, I know they will be willing to help with children. I've heard from Nancy Peterson in Kentucky, Shirley Brown in Philadelphia, Sharon Bishop in Nebraska, Tish McGonegal in Vermont, and many, many others asking what they can do to help. They can help the children who are pouring into our local schools where they have neither school supplies nor friends. I feel another mass e-mail coming on.

Friday, September 9

Dear Friends,

I have heard from National Writing Project people all over the country expressing their concern for those whose lives have been devastated by Hurricane Katrina and the aftermath. Many have asked how they can help. Of course the Red Cross and Salvation Army would welcome your contributions, but on the local TV news yesterday I heard an appeal for contributions that really touched my school teacher's heart. They were asking for help to buy school supplies, uniforms (yes, they wear uniforms here), and backpacks for children who have had to leave their homes and schools and enter schools that were not hit by the storm. Yesterday alone Lafayette Parish (where I live) registered over six hundred homeless children as new students. The number eventually climbed to around six thousand. They hope to have everyone in classrooms by Tuesday of next week. The parents of these children have no access to money to pay for school expenses since their banks are closed and ATMs non-functioning. Even if banks were available, many of the parents could not cover the expenses because they live in poverty. If you want to help these children, you can send a contribution to the Louisiana Association for the Education of Homeless Children and Youth. (I didn't know such an organization existed until yesterday.) I called them this morning, and they say they are desperate for help. They used the word "crisis."

CHAPTER 5

The Rescue Stories

A Long Trip from New Orleans
By Audrey Leonard as told by Greg Davis

The order for mass evacuation of New Orleans was issued on Sunday, just hours before Katrina made landfall. Anxiety in the city was already high, as each televised weather bulletin showed the intensifying hurricane moving inexorably towards the Louisiana coast, like a magnet being pulled by a force it couldn't resist.

Like many of the people in their neighborhood, the Prevosts, a black family living in St. Bernard Parish, heeded the instructions they were given and went outside to wait for buses that would take them out of harm's way. Meanwhile the hurricane loomed closer and closer, but no buses came. For hours they dutifully waited along with their neighbors, lined up along their street, but eventually it was apparent that to continue waiting was fruitless. The buses were not coming, but Katrina was. They returned to their homes to wait out the devastating storm.

Katrina hit, and the water quickly began to rise to dangerous levels. Realizing that they could drown in their home, they began to climb to the roof, no easy job in the middle of the raging storm. Fighting the wind and rushing waters, the father climbed a porch post to the roof, and the mother struggled to hand him one crying, screaming child at a time. Then he helped drag her up, and they clung together on the sharp, peaked roof buffeted by the frightening elements, watching the water rise to the rafters.

When the sounds of Katrina subsided, they were replaced by the sounds of screams, a chorus of cries for help. Despite the clamor of voices, the family did not see anyone when they scanned the neighboring rooftops. Their friends were trapped in their homes or attics. The ghastly screams, so loud at the beginning, slowly faded until finally all was deadly quiet.

The Prevosts, concerned that the water might soon cover their roof, decided that they had to escape. Grabbing on to a floating sheet of wood, they slowly maneuvered their way towards a two-story school, but a high fence was blocking their way. They could not go over it, and because of their inability to steer the makeshift float, they could not go around it. The father dived into the water to investigate and found a sizeable hole in the fence that might be their only hope. He instructed his wife that they would each dive under the water with a child. She should go first. The child was told to hold his breath no matter what.

The mother went under with a child tucked under one arm, but could not get through. Because she stayed under longer than expected, the husband began to fear the worst. Suddenly she popped up with the child intact. Catching her breath, she dived again, her husband behind her this time with the remaining child tucked under his arm. They made their way through the fence, across the remaining water, and into the building.

After what seemed to be an eternity, the family was picked up by helicopter and taken to dry ground where they were instructed to make their way to the Superdome. Having been without food or water for several days, the father broke into a store to pick up provisions. As they were walking towards the Superdome, two black policemen confronted them, took the provisions, and told them to keep on going. When they finally got to the Dome, seeing the bodies outside and sensing the dark and stench inside, they decided to keep walking. They were thirsty, hungry, wet, and miserable, but they were alive. They moved on.

At last they made it to I-10, where they decided to try hitchhiking and were eventually picked up by an elderly white couple. Down the highway, they were stopped near a small community by a roadblock. The car was quickly surrounded by four stereotypical, white, small-town deputies. Big-gutted and heavily armed, they began yelling, "Get the f— out of the car." Stunned and scared, they complied, the children screaming with terror. The deputies demanded that they stand spread eagle as they were frisked with guns pointed at their heads. When the officers decided the Prevost family was not a risk, they were allowed to leave, but they no longer had transportation. The frightened couple had long ago driven off in shock. The family started walking again.

After a while, a white man in a truck stopped to pick them up, offering to take them to his home in Baton Rouge. What to do? Could they trust him or could he be another threat? Too tired not to go, they climbed wearily into his truck. Their fears turned out to be groundless, as he fed them and let them shower at his home, but since he had no fresh clothes for them, they had to redress in their smelly, filthy things. Because he had heard that the Cajundome in Lafayette had set up a shelter, he agreed to drive them there. Two hours later he dropped them off, prompting Greg Davis to ask how they had gotten there at that hour of the morning as most of the evacuees had been bussed in earlier. And so their story came to be told.

A Police Officer's View
By Guy LeBreton, Lafayette City Police Department

As a police officer, I spent Wednesday night at the Cajundome as many of the displaced residents from New Orleans were brought in. I want to share my experiences.

I am ashamed to admit that when I was first notified that I would have to provide assistance and security at the shelter, my thoughts were about having to fight with angry, violent mobs coming in frustrated from their recent disaster and the treatment from rescuers and law enforcement along the way. Learning that we would have to search each person and his or her belongings for contraband, I expected more resistance.

As the first bus arrived, I noticed an obviously traumatized crowd enter. Instead of frustration and anger, I saw despair and sadness in their faces. As a security measure, officers had to invade the little sense of privacy each person had by doing thorough property searches. Not one person objected. Very few even questioned why we had to take some of their property for the safety of the group, and the ones that did understood. They were simply grateful to have a roof over their heads and services such as electricity and running water.

I saw how little these people could salvage from their lives prior to evacuating. A few had vital records, photo albums, or letters from deceased loved ones. Some even had to discard these cherished things to fill their only bag with bottles of water and crackers to survive. Little children, naive to what was occurring, had to leave all the toys and games behind, with no understanding as to why.

Each officer worked at least sixteen hours straight that night, some even longer. I know each of them felt the same compassion that I did for these people. Despite the long hours, I never heard one officer lose his temper or be disrespectful. After seeing and hearing the evacuees' devastating experiences and fight for survival, you can't be. I am proud of my fellow officers and how they handled this trying and difficult assignment.

I was particularly touched by one elderly man sitting in a chair beside the front doors watching the evacuees as they arrived. Throughout the night, he paced anxiously and asked workers repeatedly about buses coming to the shelter or taking evacuees elsewhere. His face showed despair and sadness. Eight hours later, I saw this same man huddled on the floor with his head in his hands. I asked a Red Cross volunteer why he had not yet been given a blanket and place to rest. The volunteer told me that he insisted on sitting by the door because he had been separated from his only family, his wife, and wanted nothing more than to find her again. He asked for no food, no water, no blanket, only for help in finding his wife. I pray that she survived and that they will meet again.

I awoke Thursday to reports of riots, robberies, and terrorizing in Lafayette by the evacuees. For a moment, I was ashamed of the community where I was raised and where I work. Then I realized that everyone had not seen and heard what I had. These people were physically and emotionally beaten down. They were not here to ravage Lafayette. In fact, many commented how they had been treated better here than in New Orleans. I am embarrassed that my community would foster such rumors without any evidence.

I also awoke Thursday with a new appreciation for things that I have—a home, electricity, and running water. None of these people had that. That night I put my children in their beds and kissed my wife good-night. Some of these people will never do that again.

It is time for Acadiana to embrace our fellow Louisianians in their time of need. Many of the evacuees asked immediately upon arrival about applying for jobs, finding permanent housing, and getting their children into schools. They recognized that they have been placed in a great community and wanted to become respected members of it.

I am not naive enough to say that some did not make poor choices while here. It is my job to deal with them when they made those choices. But until such a time, they deserved a helping hand. I urged my fellow Acadians not to make premature, negative assumptions about the futures of the evacuees, to allow them to develop your trust, and realize they may make our community even better. Remember, for many of them, their pride was all they had left.

The Man in Blue Pants
Source: *Michelle Wright*

Sometimes people are not what we think they are. Volunteer Michelle Wright had her assumptions challenged when a huge man arrived on one of the early buses from New Orleans. His clothes were filthy and his scowl was threatening. Her suspicions only increased when she saw that he wore two diamond watches and a large diamond necklace. Everything about him seemed to fit the stereotype of an inner-city drug dealer or worse.

The man approached Michelle on the third floor and said he had blisters on his feet because of his shoes. Feeling more than a little threatened, she took him to the second-floor clinic and to the showers. In the meantime she looked for some clothes for him, which was not easy since he wore size 3XL. All she could find was a pair of blue drawstring pants with colorful flowers on each leg. With some trepidation she gave them to him, and to her surprise she discovered that he was overjoyed. He came out of the shower area and gave her a huge hug and smile. Sometimes people are not what we think they are.

Lost and Found
Source: *Michelle Wright*

A middle-of-the-night arrival of dozens of buses carrying exhausted, distraught evacuees would have thrown any shelter into confusion. The night they arrived at the Cajundome from New Orleans was typical. Doctors and nurses threw themselves into triage efforts, arena staffers ran to find towels for the lines of people waiting for showers, and security struggled to maintain an orderly registration process. In the midst of the swirling activity, a little woman asked for help for her mother. Because there were no wheelchairs, volunteer Michelle Wright asked two residents to carry the older woman to a chair where a nurse could examine her. When the nurse discovered the woman had had no food for days, had missed her dialysis treatment, and was on a feeding tube, she immediately sent her by ambulance to University Medical Center.

The two women were part of a group of thirty Baudoin family members who had gone through the storm together at a grandson's house. When the water started coming in, one of the men broke into a storehouse that had a second story where they took refuge for several days, waving from the roof to get help. A Coast Guard helicopter rescued the elderly woman, her daughter, two granddaughters, and a ten-day-old infant. The rest of the family was left with a promise that someone would come back to get them. Those who were evacuated were dropped off at Interstate 10 and Causeway, where they waited in the sun for the rest of the family to join them. They never came, and eventually those who had made it out boarded a bus for Lafayette.

At the Cajundome, the Baudoins began to feel safe again. The doctors at UMC diagnosed the elderly woman with severe dehydration and hospitalized her. Her daughter stayed with her. If they could only connect with those they left behind in New Orleans, all might be well. Suddenly everything was reversed. Relief was replaced with new anxieties and fears. While the daughter was at the Cajundome to pick up some personal items, her mother disappeared. She was no longer at University Medical Center, but hospital personnel did not know where she was. Calls went out to all hospitals in the area, and she was finally found late that night in a newly opened facility in Youngsville. She had been sent to Breaux Bridge for dialysis, and because she was so ill, she was not returned to UMC, but UMC had neglected to make a record of the transfer.

In the meantime, the Lafayette branch of the family kept looking for the New Orleans contingent. As it turned out, the Coast Guard never came back to pick up the remaining family members, and they were forced to stay where they were for two more days until an Army helicopter rescued them. They were subsequently sent to a shelter on a military base near San Antonio, Texas. Joe Baudoin said, "Those people treated me like I was a king."

Eventually everyone managed to get to Lafayette, and the family was reunited. Joe found a job, and the hospital hired one of the women. The infant was temporarily adopted by a woman in Lafayette to get her out of the Cajundome, and the grandmother remained in the hospital. They had moved into new lives.

A Family Separated, then Reunited
Source: Michelle Wright

Life does not stop for hurricanes. People still get sick, have babies, eat, and sleep. One New Orleans family was made acutely aware of how life's events go on despite cataclysmic natural disturbances. When

Katrina arrived, they had a child at Tulane University Hospital who was suffering from a brain tumor. When the hospital had to be emptied, they were not allowed to accompany her. Instead, they were sent to the Cajundome in Lafayette and were told their daughter was sent to Women and Children's Hospital in Houston, where she was scheduled to have a serious surgical procedure at 6:00 A.M. They were terribly upset about the separation and desperate to find a way to get to Houston in time for the surgery.

At midnight, local volunteer Michelle Wright started trying to help them find a way to get to Houston and, in the process, discovered that there is no Women and Children's Hospital in Houston. Calling medical centers all over the city in an effort to find the couple's daughter, Wright eventually located her at Texas Children's Hospital, where a nurse said they were going to do the procedure as scheduled. She said if the parents could get there, the hospital would take care of them.

At this point American Red Cross representative Colleen Brothers made an executive decision that was not entirely in compliance with Red Cross procedures. She asked two young Red Cross workers with a rental car to take the couple to Houston. In preparation, Wright called the Louisiana State Police and explained the need for haste. Their officers advised her that the driver should turn on his hazard lights and go as safely as possible with heightened speed. While they were en route, a sheriff in the western part of Louisiana intervened with help from Acadian Ambulance, which took them on to Houston in an ambulance. With everyone's help, the couple managed to arrive in time for their child's surgery.

Efforts on Behalf of the Dead
By Pam DeVille

One of the saddest of stories coming out of St. Bernard Parish is that of a young girl and her mother who arrived at the Cajundome five days after Katrina struck. The girl's father had had a heart attack during the hurricane. She and her mother dragged his dead body through water for two days to get to Plaquemine. Finally they found an overpass that was above the flooding and sat on it with his body for two more days. Finally a helicopter came that would take his body away, but the mother and daughter waited yet another day before being rescued themselves. They finally found the man's body in a morgue. They had one overwhelming concern—that he be treated with respect.

A Shaky Arrival
Source: Michelle Wright

On Friday night after Katrina landed, the Cajundome was notified to expect people from the Morial Convention Center in New Orleans. Volunteers stood in front of the building to help people off the buses. One of the first to come down the steps was a big man who was shaking and asking for a glass of water. Then two girls, ten-year-old Latisha and seventeen-year-old Mona, appeared, both of them hysterical. They had not eaten in days, but they were terrified of entering the shelter because it was a convention center, and they thought it would be like the one in New Orleans. Greg Davis let them go to the head of the line for showers, then took them to a quiet place and gave them pizza.

There was good cause for their hysteria. Latisha kept saying, "The alligator almost got me," and making wavy motions with her hands to indicate how it moved through the water. Then she remembered the snakes that came to her house in New Orleans seeking high ground.

The girls were cousins who had been separated from their family when the mother who had accompanied them turned away to help another child, a paraplegic who had been the casualty of a random shooting near her home in one of the New Orleans housing developments. Latisha and Mona had made their way alone through the flooded streets to the convention center because it was on high ground. When they arrived there, they saw a dead body and a dead baby. The older girl refused to sleep because she had heard that girls were being raped, and she was determined to protect her younger cousin.

At one point a policeman let them go into a little grocery store on Canal Street and get food and water, but they were afraid because they saw the police shoot two men who were taking large items. Latisha remembered that the saddest thing was the foreign people who were huddled together. They couldn't speak English, and they were afraid to go in. She got a honey bun and a Coke and gave them the Coke. The police were telling people to take cars if they could, try not to damage them, but use them to get out.

Finally a bus came, and the girls joined the crowd of people who stormed it. They were about to leave when they saw their mothers with their grandmother through the window of the bus. Eventually other family members were located in Houston, and the family was reunited.

PART III

The Relief Phase

Give what you have. To someone, it may be better than you dare to think.
— Henry Wadsworth Longfellow

CHAPTER 6

Making a Community

Although "normal" was never a term that described the fifty-eight days of the Cajundome's mega-shelter existence, sometimes life there fell into a pattern that grew to be familiar and almost comfortable. Between crises, the regularity of services, such as meals and laundry pick-up—the stuff of everyday living—made the public nature of the evacuees' existence more bearable. The small areas inhabited by families took on their personalities. One might have a television set playing most of the day; another could be piled high with stuffed animals. They were small replicas of homes and, as such, were guarded by those who lived in them. The fact that there was no violence in the Cajundome, not even a scuffle, is due in large part to the regularity and predictability of what went on there. It was as close to normal as an arena turned shelter could ever be.

Rising to cope with the crisis demanded courage, energy, and ingenuity, but coping with the ongoing relief efforts as the weeks dragged on required a different set of skills and abilities. The increased demand on the facilities significantly added to the workload of the Cajundome staff, which began to fall into a routine, a routine that to Bill Blanchet, assistant director of finance and operations, felt like being in hyper drive.

One of the people who was critical to large-scale coping was Pam DeVille, normally the Cajundome's assistant director in charge of marketing and booking. During the shelter operation she wore many hats, not to mention an earpiece that allowed her to take endless phone calls. Its ring tone was the aria sung by the Queen of the Night in Mozart's opera *The Magic Flute,* a fact that seemed appropriate in this situation. She was a queen working magic night and day.

On August 30, DeVille assumed responsibility for maintaining morale among the staff and networking with other agencies, those working in the Cajundome and those outside it. For example, she became the chief liaison between the Cajundome and the city-parish government, city-parish president Joey Durel, the Department of Motor Vehicles, FEMA, the Red Cross, Dr. Paul Azar and other medical personnel, and many others. In that capacity she dealt with constant inquiries; worked long and unusual hours; met with volunteers, Red Cross workers, and officials; and solved problems for evacuees. In the final weeks of the shelter, she and her secretary, Heidi Champagne, were responsible for making arrangements for many of the evacuees to leave the Cajundome and move into other quarters. Through it all, she remained sunny and bright, defusing potentially ugly moments and sometimes just making people laugh.

Operations director Phil Ashurst turned his immediate attention to a very different but equally critical area, sanitation. Daily cleaning required three crews of twenty-five people each, many of them residents of the shelter, working twenty-four hours a day. To prevent the spread of disease, each bathroom stall was cleaned three times in a row, several times a day, to be sure all bacteria had been killed. The crews called their work "hyper cleaning." It was not without its hazards. After an employee was stuck with a needle when picking up towels, Ashurst established policies for avoiding contamination by drug needles. From then on the cleaning staff used steel tongs and puncture-proof gloves, not their bare hands. The clinic posed problems of dealing with bio-medical waste. Everything had to be disinfected. Ashurst brought in Don Guidry from Our Lady of Lourdes Hospital to give instructions in hospital-cleaning techniques and contacted cruise ships about how they handle outbreaks of illness. Ashurst, already well-known for his meticulous record keeping, made more lists, of cleaning procedures, safety tips, and sanitation techniques.

The huge demand for telephones was served by Cox Communications, Bell South, Cingular, and Centennial Wireless, which made phones available to different agencies and residents. Initially, phone service was sketchy because the lines were out of New Orleans, but after about two weeks they began to work efficiently. Cox Communications provided six phones for the residents to use at no charge. Two were in the Convention Center at the south concession stand, and four were in the Cajundome across from stand 117. They also provided an additional twenty-three numbers to various locations for many different entities, such as agencies providing transportation and housing, and brought in more lines for the Red Cross and other agencies such as the Department of Labor and Job Services. All together, there were more than sixty temporary phone numbers added at the facility for this operation, many of which were used for only a few weeks, but others for the entire stay. Many changed location several times during the sheltering operation, which meant that either the Cajundome staff would have to move the lines or UCI or Cox would come back to do so.

Computers, too, were needed by everyone. At the outset Ashton Langlinais, president and CEO of WOW Technologies, had linked the various agencies by a fiber ring that tied everyone together, a move that significantly improved internal communication. For example, the Red Cross had thirteen locations at the Cajundome, and the fiber ring linked them all. The system spanned both the Cajundome and the Convention Center and had a wireless microwave link to surrounding, outlying areas, such as to the National Guard. Langlinais incorporated Voice over Internet Protocol (VoIP) phones and installed ten cellular phone repeaters from Cingular for emergency communications. He also installed a wireless link and high-end surveillance. The campus-wide network he installed for the medical staff was eventually moved to University Medical Center when the clinic was transferred there. Langlinais was able to accomplish so much quickly because he already had equipment on-site. He had twelve people working for him, four of whom were working twelve- to fourteen-hour days on this job. Cisco Systems donated around three hundred thousand dollars of installed equipment.

Lafayette Coming Together, a fairly new organization, was instrumental in getting technological assistance to the residents. Formed in March 2005 to address the "digital divide" in Lafayette, its mission is to provide better access to technology for the underserved in the community. Its presence at the Cajundome was initiated by David Goodwyn, who realized that LCT's expertise and equipment could be of help to those who would be sheltered there. He mobilized the effort on September 1, three days after Hurricane Katrina, and had it operational by the morning of September 2. It remained functional until the computers were removed on October 15.

LCT volunteers provided Internet access on up to twenty computers and technological assistance to residents for a variety of needs. A great many requested help with filing applications with FEMA, but others were looking for jobs, housing, and missing friends and relatives. They were communicating through e-mail, getting news about their hometowns, seeing posthurricane aerial photos of their neighborhoods, searching for hotel accommodations, researching living conditions in other areas of the country, and entertaining themselves with games and music videos. LCT also provided one-on-one assistance to residents who had minimal or no computer skills, including in many cases giving crash courses in the use of the technology. Four (VoIP) phones were available in the center for residents to use to call long distance at no charge. This service was particularly valuable in the early days of the shelter when there was no other public-phone access. At times the volunteers simply served as unofficial sympathetic listeners for evacuees who needed to talk things out, explain themselves, and engage in the sort of conversation that helps people understand their situation.

Layne and John St. Julien served as shift leaders and organizers of the LCT effort. They helped organize the volunteers, met with community leaders from both Zydetec and the Chamber of Commerce, which played significant roles in helping find volunteers for the effort, and worked with the staff of the Cajundome. At the Lafayette Coming Together Computer Center, they were responsible for setting up and taking down the equipment, opening the Computer Center at the beginning of their shift, soliciting volunteers from among those already at work in the shelter, making sure the residents had fair access to the equipment, giving advice about how to find information online, monitoring use of the VoIP phones, and at shift's end, making sure the room was ready for the next shift. They also aided residents with filing FEMA applications online and helped them locate relatives, jobs, and housing.

The number of residents served is difficult to estimate because the size of the crowd varied, and many people made multiple visits to the computer room. The center was open three shifts per day (morning, afternoon, and night), providing at least nine hours of service a day, seven days a week, for six weeks. At times it was open for additional hours due to increased demand. An educated guess would be that residents made more than four thousand visits to the Computer Center.

LCT's greatest success was in making Internet access quickly available to the residents. It allowed them to file for FEMA assistance days before FEMA was set up in the Cajundome and, once they had filed, to check on the status of their applications online, a service that FEMA did not offer in those first few days. In addition, online resources provided by LCT made looking for family members much easier. John St. Julien gives credit for the effectiveness of the LCT volunteers to the spontaneous way in which they worked. They were not burdened by having rules or structured plans that did not suit the nature of the crisis. They knew what they wanted to do, though at the outset they were not clear about the precise methods they would use. That stance allowed them to be flexible and quickly respond to people's needs. Throughout its time at the Cajundome, LCT operated with a loose, informal structure that provided opportunities for it to be effective in ways that more bureaucratic organizations could not be.

Feeding thousands of people three well-balanced, attractive, and good-tasting meals each day posed different challenges than those presented by technology needs. Food service was especially important in Acadiana, where eating well is one of life's greatest pleasures. Meals from cans were not acceptable. Instead, Mark Tyrrell and chef Gilbert DeCourt worked together to provide a traditional breakfast and a lunch of salad, a hot entrée, and a vegetable. Dinner was the same without a salad. Tyrrell made it a policy to tolerate no alcohol and to serve ample quantities of water. Typical breakfast offerings included grits, scrambled eggs, bacon, sausage, biscuits, fresh fruit, juice, and milk. Lunch and dinner entrées included chicken à la king, beef stroganoff, chicken and sausage sauce piquant, shrimp Creole, barbecued brisket, sausage jambalaya, meatballs and marinara sauce, Salisbury steak, chicken-fried steak, and barbecue and baked chicken.

The Cajundome kitchen was designed to prepare food for two thousand people. At its peak, the shelter served almost seven thousand. The total number of meals served over the eight-week period was around

427,000. Tyrrell had a staff of seven, plus some part-time people. To alleviate the shortage of workers, the Cajundome hired some of the residents. The Cajundome staff, supervisors, and volunteers—thirty of them at the Cajundome, twenty at the Convention Center—served the food at attractively appointed tables using catering serving dishes, which were a marked contrast to the large plastic dispensers used by the Red Cross. The staff worked with the Red Cross to keep the snack bar open as well.

Tyrrell brought in Lisa Owen, a nutritionist at Lafayette General Hospital, to advise him about meeting the food needs of so many people, some of them on restricted diets. He also contacted the health department and the Centers for Disease Control and Prevention for advice on preventing illness. The special dietary needs of around two hundred residents, twenty-five of them diabetics, were met. The local health department, the CDC, and state authorities all inspected the Cajundome kitchen and gave it their highest ratings.

DeMarcus Thomas, a coach and teacher at Harrisville State College and Iberia Parish Schools, arrived on the second day that the Cajundome was a shelter. Greg Davis, recognizing the need for physical activity among the residents, especially the children and young people, asked Thomas to create recreational programs to alleviate boredom and inactivity. Thomas quickly arranged venues for basketball, flag football, horseshoes, and foosball. He contacted local businesses in an effort to provide a fun jump, table games, and even a trip to Kart Ranch, a local amusement area. In all, he organized ten different teams with twelve children and young people on each team.

His activities served the irresistible pull to normalcy shared by all evacuees.

A number of church choirs and performing groups, such as bands, singers, and dancers, presented entertainment for anyone who wanted to attend. The director of the Acadiana Symphony Orchestra Conservatory provided fifteen interactive music sessions for children of all ages.

During the relief phase, the sheriff's office, police officers, and National Guard were charged with maintaining order and security and providing for the safety of those living and working in the facility. Their duties were difficult because the Cajundome was built with multiple entrances and exits to get people in and out quickly. Guards maintained positions at all points of entrance and egress to control access to the facility. Although the security personnel were understaffed during the first week, they still met and exceeded expectations.

Written house rules that were already in place before the Cajundome became a shelter remained. For example, guns and drugs were banned, and there was zero tolerance for disturbances. When it became a shelter, security personnel found themselves additionally challenged with enforcing Red Cross shelter rules, which ban all sharp objects, cigarette lighters, scissors, and cameras. In addition, there was a 10:00 P.M. curfew, although separate television areas were provided for those not ready to sleep. Even so, sometimes residents who did not want to go to bed at that time disturbed those who wanted to be quiet. Quiet time, which ran from 1:00 A.M. to 6:00 A.M., was often violated.

Despite rumors to the contrary, infractions of law and house rules were minor at the Cajundome and the Convention Center during the relief phase. Sheriff's deputy Kip Judice and local police made around one hundred arrests, none of them for significant acts of violence. Nevertheless, wild stories circulated throughout the city that roving bands of looters had robbed Shooters Supply of all its weapons, held up a bank, and broken into several homes on Foreman Street. Gun sales went up, some schools were locked down, and several businesses closed. The sheriff's office's phones were busy with inquiries. Even after Joey Durel, the police department, and others denied the reports, some people continued to believe they were true, asserting that civic authorities were covering up the crimes to prevent panic in the streets.

Gangs made an attempt to establish territories inside the building, and for a short period of time did not allow anyone who was not from their own neighborhoods to use certain bathrooms, halls, or stairs. They practiced intimidation, used drugs, caused fights, and even one shooting, which took place in the Duson area. The Lafayette security people did not recognize gang members at the outset, but the first National Guard contingent on site, which was from Washington, D.C., immediately noticed the behavior. As a result, they placed two guards on the leaders wherever they went, resulting in several arrests that accounted for 70 percent of all that were made. After being notified of the gang activity, Judice challenged their domination and broke them up by housing them in separate areas, after which there were fewer problems. Northside High School, which enrolled a large number of suspected gang members, called to ask for help. The New Orleans Police Department faxed a warrant for the arrest of the leader of the group.

In the end, not one violent crime—stabbing, shooting, or beating—was committed in the Cajundome. Some people who gave the Cajundome as their address were arrested off property, but on-site the environment was generally orderly and peaceful. The absence of violent crime at this facility was evidence of the success of the program, considering that before Katrina New Orleans had the highest per capita homicide rate in the nation and many of the people brought to the Cajundome were from the most violent areas of that city. The mayor and sheriff used the media to counteract the rumors and thus quieted Lafayette's fears. Judice gives credit for the lack of violence to the law-enforcement people and the residents who were flexible and patient enough to give security personnel time to get a good plan in place. The plan carried them through.

Those who did violate the law had to leave the facility. Anyone committing a rule infraction, recorded by a hole punch in the offender's ID tag, received a verbal reprimand and a warning that a second offense would result in expulsion. If a person under the age of eighteen was evicted, one parent had to go with him or her. If the person was a parent or guardian, the whole family had to go. Judice told the story of one boy who repeatedly broke rules. Though his mother struggled to keep him in line, she was no match for gang members from New Orleans who were influencing him. Finally he and his mother were both evicted. Members of the Cajundome staff contributed money to pay for a hotel for them until the Foundation for Hope managed to send them to South Carolina, where the boy's behavior improved considerably once he was out of the reach of the bad influences around him.

Most security actions during the relief phase occurred as the result of long hours that led to short tempers easily provoked by the occasional flippant remark. Police and staff worked sixteen-hour shifts for extended periods of time with no days off because every agency needed security. The situation was made even more stressful by the knowledge that the residents could take over if they wanted to.

Fortunately, tensions did not occur among the police, sheriff's office, and National Guard. All three agencies agreed at the outset that the sheriff's office would be in charge of everything inside the Cajundome, the police would be in charge of everything outside the building, and the National Guard would move between the two. There were some communication issues initially, but the people involved quickly learned to let each other know what they were doing.

At night, security officers continued to maintain a presence at the front entrance for those who had left for the day and were returning. They increased patrols on the perimeters to protect cars and run off undesirable people. Because of reports of nighttime theft, they tried to keep a high profile by moving around the facility on all levels during the curfew hours.

Although the sheriff's office designated Deputy Judice to be in charge of security, the staff of the Cajundome also assumed responsibility for maintaining an orderly routine and environment. A representative was on-site twenty-four hours a day to see that curfews and meal times were observed.

A prime example of the staff's concern for the well-being of the residents was the evacuation drill held on September 30, three nights before Hurricane Rita made landfall. Initially the residents, remembering their negative experiences at the Superdome, were reluctant to participate. They were afraid that they might be subjected to similar mistreatment. Ashurst, in concert with Judice, the National Guard, police, and other staff members, devised a plan to get 1,200 people calmly and quickly out of the Cajundome and onto buses for evacuation. Assembled on the second level of the building, the residents in each section received tickets that corresponded to numbered buses. Each section had a chaperone. A person could take only what would fit in his or her lap, leaving everything else to be locked up. Each convoy of five buses was to be accompanied by a police car, an ambulance, and a Humvee. When the evacuation became a reality, the plan operated, according to FEMA representative Tricia Schaefer, like "a well-oiled machine."

The Cajundome could not have operated at the high level it sustained for the fifty-eight days had it not been for the self-motivated and highly organized volunteers who showed up to work. In addition to medical personnel, around 125 people gave of their time, energy, and skills to assist in the rescue, relief, and relocation activities at the shelter. Most of them were individuals who simply felt drawn to help. They did not necessarily have experience with such efforts, but they had skills and knowledge that could be useful and that they were willing to contribute. Working sometimes in concert with the Red Cross and sometimes alone, they were responsible for a wide variety of services.

Celeste White and Guy Ellison set up the Information Desk in the lobby of the Cajundome. It provided data about everything from the times of church services to how to get Social Security checks to where to find opportunities to relocate. Because they were repeatedly asked the same questions, White compiled a list of frequently asked questions. When she did not know the answer to a question, she made phone calls to find people who did. For example, she called Social Security, the food stamp office, and other agencies that evacuees needed to access. She made a sketch of the Cajundome and found Lafayette maps for them to use. She made a vital-information sheet that explained how to use local transportation. She even put signs on the walls to help people find their way around the building. To keep the Information Desk operating, White compiled a list of people who could work. Trying to keep the desk open twenty-four hours a day, she had a night worker and a day worker and two retirees serving eight-hour shifts, although it was difficult to keep trained volunteers on the job.

Leslie Sandlin worked with White and Ellison from the beginning. Her job was to make daily reports and update the data. Questions typical of those she received included: How do I find the unemployment office? Where can I pick up my prescription? How do I get to the pharmacy? Where do you sign up for school? Where can I get some reading glasses? How do I get my Social Security check? What can I do with my children?

Dan Hawthorne arrived every morning at seven to make about fifty copies of informative materials to hand out to people during the day. In addition, he answered questions about the entire shelter experience: clothing, food, Red Cross assistance, transportation, food stamps, FEMA. When needed, he acted as a runner by going out and getting needed information. He was committed to being patient and clear while working one-on-one with clients. In return, he said, they were appreciative and grateful. They often asked his name, and he would simply show his ID tag that said, "Local Volunteer."

James Proctor described himself as a problem solver and a decision maker. With that in mind he roamed the shelter to determine what was needed. He made on-the-spot decisions so that problems did not have to be sent higher. He arrived wanting to do a daily news sheet, which turned into *The Daily Dome,* a newsletter operating with two reporters, one a resident, the other a local. They collected information and published the daily news on a computer. Proctor also wanted to install playground equipment, a magazine cart, and several other recreational items, but he mainly worked with Red Cross personnel to accomplish their goals. He used skills developed over a lifetime to be effective in this situation.

Michelle Wright, like most of the individual volunteers, assigned herself responsibilities for helping wherever there seemed to be a need. She came when she heard an all-call for volunteers to go to the Cajundome beginning Tuesday afternoon, August 30. Much of her time was spent organizing supplies and distributing goods to newly arrived evacuees. In the course of handing out pillows and blankets early on, she was reprimanded by Red Cross members. Her actions violated their policy of not giving out items unless there are enough for all who need them. But with a will typical of the volunteers, she continued to distribute them. She and her husband raised money from Lafayette citizens for specific projects, requested supplies—which came by overnight delivery from Americares, a private foundation—and bought pillows and blankets from local stores for evacuees' use.

Denise Melancon, director of the Acadiana Symphony Orchestra Conservatory, volunteered to present music time three times a week from September 8 through October 20, fifteen classes in all. Children of all ages were invited to participate in Orff training (marching in rhythm), read books, sing, and compete for prizes. Two evacuees volunteered to assist Melancon. Most of the sessions were held in the front part of the arena and three took place in the Convention Center. Around twenty children and their parents attended each session. A year later Melancon continued to hear from the children who were touched by her efforts. Now scattered across the country, they still send her e-mails to tell her that they loved the music.

After Hurricane Katrina, the Lafayette Parish Schools moved quickly to enroll children in local schools. School buses were made available to pick up and deliver children living in the shelter. The Louisiana Association for the Education of Homeless Children and Youth accepted donations of money and supplies to provide uniforms, backpacks, and school supplies for the new students.

Despite these efforts, many of the children at the Cajundome arrived after the deadline for enrolling in local schools had passed. In addition, those who would be in the shelter for only a brief period of time did not want to start school and withdraw in a week or so. To meet their needs Keith Bartlett, a displaced New Orleans teacher, organized TAPS (Transitional Academic Program for Students), a kindergarten through twelfth-grade school that met in a ballroom on the second floor of the Convention Center. The school was funded by Lafayette Parish Schools, and supplies came from a variety of sources. Chad Zeringue of the Chamber of Commerce and Patrick Landry of the University of Louisiana at Lafayette provided twelve new computers. The local school district installed a copy machine and supplied teaching materials. The staff of TAPS consisted of three certified teachers and several paraprofessionals, all of them displaced from their own schools by Hurricane Katrina. The assistant coordinator was in charge of student behavior. Bartlett served as chief administrator.

The school day was organized with grades kindergarten through fourth meeting from 8:00 A.M. until 11:30 A.M. and fifth through twelfth from noon to 3:30 P.M. The staff tried to maintain grade classifications, while being sensitive to varying levels of ability and preparation. Consequently, some groups mixed grade levels. The curriculum was organized in three seventy-minute blocks focused on language arts, math, and enrichment (art, study skills, physical education, and technology). Outside agencies such as the Acadiana Arts Council and the Children's Museum of Acadiana agreed to provide field experiences for the third block. One day nurses came by to talk about nutrition, stress, and even health careers. They gave hand massages to the children.

The pedagogy at TAPS was primarily interactive, with the children and teachers seated around large tables. With around sixty students, the pupil-teacher ratio was approximately twelve to one. The children were neatly dressed, most of the girls wearing bows in their hair. Their faces had life in them again, reinforced by hugs and smiles from the teachers. It was an environment the children understood, one where they knew what to expect, a place they felt safe.

TAPS lasted three days, then dissolved in the evacuation of all Cajundome residents in the face of Hurricane Rita.

One area in which the university made a significant contribution to the relief efforts was in health care. Under the direction of Jill Laroussini, who teaches the clinical portion of a community/mental psychiatric course in ULL's College of Nursing and Allied Health Professions, nursing students aided countless numbers of evacuees by checking blood pressures, listening to their stories, and helping them deal with their grief. The nursing students worked to identify those who needed prescriptions refilled and contacted local pharmacies for them. At the Convention Center they helped elderly people transfer to appropriate health-care facilities, such as rehabilitation centers or nursing homes, or simply to join family members outside the storm-impacted area.

During the relief period, the production/setup department of the Cajundome assisted with everything from emptying trash cans, sanitizing areas, unstopping toilets, and clearing storage areas to setting up pipe and drape and installing television sets for entertainment. Its crews looked for abandoned bedding and unloaded supply trucks from FEMA distribution centers, churches, and other organizations. They assisted in relocating residents to other areas as necessary, picked up broken cots and sanitized the good ones, wrapped biohazard bedding in plastic sheeting, and handled the storage and disposal of medical waste. They even turned on a big-screen TV and activated a listening-assistance system so that the residents could tune their radios to a specific frequency to listen to what was being broadcast on the video wall. During the first week, someone from the production department was on duty around the clock. As the relief phase moved on, the night staff was reduced, but still they seemed to be everywhere.

Throughout much of the relief phase funding remained a concern. Initially there was no contract signed with FEMA or the Red Cross and no commitment of support from the state or city, leaving the Cajundome with hope but no assurance of where the money to cover its costs would come from. At the same time, the Cajundome was making no money and a $900,000 contract with Chevron-Mobile was lost. Nevertheless, the governing commission never questioned the expenditures. In fact, it expended its available funds within the first three weeks of the shelter operation. Recognizing that the shelter would be closed without outside assistance, an agreement was reached whereby FEMA advanced $6 million to the City of Lafayette to be disbursed by the city-parish government to the commission.

CHAPTER 7

Spaces and Places

The layouts of the Cajundome and Convention Center changed constantly throughout the fifty-eight days they served as shelters. Services and booths had to be moved to accommodate the varying needs and numbers of the residents. For most of that time, however, the major areas of activity involved the lobby, arena, outer hallways of the Cajundome, the open area between the two buildings, and the two floors of the convention center.

The lobby served as headquarters for many agencies and services. The main entrance led first to a registration and identification checkpoint, then to security check-in through metal detectors and an area for searching of all parcels. To the immediate left of the security check-in was a station for paging people. To the immediate right was a stand furnishing soft drinks, fruit, and snacks. Directly across from it was an information desk. Staffed with volunteers available to answer questions, the desk provided telephone numbers, maps, agency information, and other helpful materials. The volunteer desk was to the right, and people lined up behind it for access to the post office. On the left side of the lobby was the laundry drop-off station. Running across the back of the lobby were stations providing Red Cross First Aid and Mental Health Counseling, a diabetes clinic, identification tags, and a wide variety of toiletries. Items from the snack bar, which was open most of the time, and the toiletries were free.

For most of the fifty-eight days of sheltering, the doors behind the lobby's service stations led directly to the arena, which housed the sleeping and meal areas. The number and arrangement of cots varied with the requirements of the people needing them. FEMA, Foundation for Hope, and Red Cross Assistance were located along the east side of the arena, although these agencies moved several times. The far end of the arena led to eleven men's showers and eleven women's showers, with hot and cold running water and privacy curtains to allow people to dress. Twenty-nine in-house showers were also available for use. Areas furnished with computers and telephones—courtesy of Cingular and Cox Communications—were available for residents to send and read e-mail, file FEMA applications (a process later moved to the FEMA area), and make calls.

Several special-interest areas were set up in the circular hallways surrounding the arena. A storage space was converted into a nursery for children ages two through eight. On a rotating basis, forty children at a time were allowed access to television, books, board games, and toys. It was staffed by members of the Pastor's Resource Council and supervised by Nate Smith, the Red Cross person in charge of recreation. For older children, a teen facility was constructed with a big-screen TV, video-games center, outside area with basketball goals, and a study area. Even a hair-care area was set up for volunteers and residents to use. An

MAP OF CAJUNDOME SHELTER

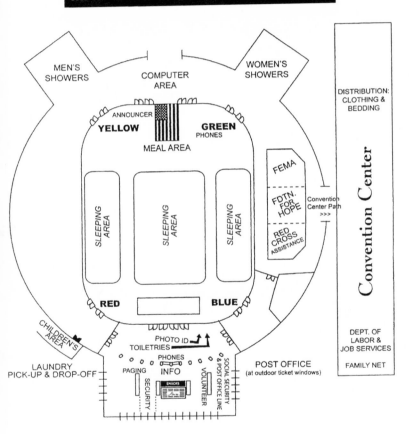

entertainment stage was placed outside between the Cajundome and Convention Center. A basketball league of evacuees also played there, sporting their own jerseys and shorts.

The Convention Center was the hub of distribution efforts. After registering, residents went there to pick up clothes, bed linens, and towels. For a brief period of time a Convention Center ballroom housed TAPS, the Transitional Academic Program for Students. On the first floor Family Net and the Department of Labor and Job Services were available to residents.

Celeste White drew up the following map of the layout of the facilities.

CHAPTER 8

A Reporter's Notebook

Saturday, September 10

The Play Day was hot, hot, hot. The good news is that so many people and organizations set up booths and tents to give the kids a holiday. Snacks and treats were ample and free. Smiles and hugs abundant.

The Acadiana Writing Project had a tent set up and was prepared to help the kids write some "paste-pot poetry." However, for some time hardly any children showed up, just the occasional little girl or boy, usually accompanied by a parent. Finally the teachers who were hosting the event realized that the kids had no transportation from the Cajundome. Their families had no cars, and the city and school buses wouldn't transport them because of insurance and legal problems. At that point some of the teachers got in their own cars, drove to the Cajundome and "checked out" children on their own responsibility. Each adult could have four children. Suddenly the tent was full of children, mostly solemn faced and big eyed, at least at first. Only a few wanted to write or draw. What they wanted was to be held, to be patted and hugged. There were plenty of willing volunteers for that duty.

Ice-cream sandwiches kept appearing from somewhere. The hot day melted them quickly, and lots of black faces were smeared with white ice cream. Then the smiles began to appear. Late that afternoon the teachers took pictures, gave a few last hugs, and put the children back in their cars to return them to the over-crowded Cajundome, to them a place full of fears, threats, and strangers.

Sunday, September 11

The churches in Lafayette are working night and day to provide meals, lodging, supplies—whatever is needed—for the people pouring through the city. My own church provides an evening meal for whoever shows up, and we are all getting to be good at cooking in large quantities. Volunteers appear ready to drive people to Alexandria or to the pharmacy. Such generosity of spirit is a powerful thing to see.

Monday, September 12

Today I got a call from Pam DeVille at the Cajundome. She says that Greg Davis has asked for someone to document all that is going on there, and apparently the university gave my name as a possibility. It would be interesting. Since all this began I have speculated about what I could do to be part of the effort, and perhaps this is it.

Wednesday, September 14

I am here. I am inside the Cajundome, wearing my official badge around my neck. I even have a parking pass to flash so that I can get round the security guard and park within a mile of the offices. I have set up my laptop in the middle of the administrative offices, using an unoccupied but very visible space. It is not only visible, but it is unavoidable. Everyone who walks through goes by me. It is the catbird seat. I should be able to see and hear everything that goes on.

It has been fifteen days since Katrina hit. The Cajundome has been in operation as a shelter for fourteen days. It still teems with people. To the casual observer there seem to be more volunteers than evacuees. The mood among the volunteers this morning is upbeat. Even the National Guard troops that operate security at the entrance are polite and friendly. The Red Cross professionals and volunteers go out of their way to smile and be approachable. The police at the first entrance are polite. Maybe it is still early in the day, a time before people are tired and frustrated. I don't know. I'll have to wait and see.

Looking outside, I can see that the driveway in front of the Dome is filled with vehicles: military trucks, Acadian Ambulance, transit vans, police cars. Long lines of bright blue Port-o-Lets stretch away from the drive. There are handwritten signs posted on every surface announcing everything from where to get food and jobs to colorful but bedraggled good wishes from the seventh graders at Sts. Leo-Seton School. They say, "We are praying for you." The arena's ticket windows have become the post office. An obscure handwritten sheet of paper says, "To pick up your scripts from CVS, please go to. . ." Will anybody see it? A more official printed announcement tells people how to get duplicate drivers' licenses and food stamps. They will have to take a van that leaves at the top of every hour.

Outside the Dome people sit and stare into the distance. A van picks up people in wheelchairs. I don't know where they're going. Others stand and talk. A table with a sign identifying the young people behind it as working for an organization called Compassion is off to the side. Nobody seems to be asking for their services. I can't tell the difference between the Red Cross professionals and volunteers. Are the pros designated by the Red Cross vests some people are wearing?

There are three entrance checkpoints into the Dome. The first is manned by local police. They look bored. The second is checked by National Guardsmen, who make sure you use hand sanitizer before entering. They are polite and friendly. Between them is a table of three Red Cross people vetting volunteers, checking to see that they carry no diseases and have not been exposed to anything contagious. The third checkpoint takes you to the National Guard again, where you go through the same process required at the airport—walk through a metal detector, put carried items in a tray for examination, and get checked over by a second metal detector.

Friday, September 16

I've never been in a war, but I think this must be what it's like to be there, witness to the noblest efforts and basest instincts, the most generous attitudes and deeply suspicious ones, hope struggling with despair.

The performances go on. We have bands and choirs and for the coming weekend a barbecue followed by a football game at Cajun Field. To read about all the entertainment one would think the Cajundome was a holiday resort, but when you look about and see the dispirited faces, you know this is no vacation. It is more like finding oneself lost without a compass or a signpost. They don't know what comes next.

Saturday, September 17

In the lobby of the Cajundome there are tables for

everything. Large, handwritten signs have arrows that point to the diabetes clinic or label the table for mental-health counseling. There are posted rules of behavior and notices about AA meetings, NA meetings, free haircuts, and job opportunities.

A large counter is full of food, and a bin holds iced bottles of water. When I arrived people were eating breakfast: scrambled eggs, sausage, biscuits, and coffee. It was hearty fare and looked good. Smelled good, too. What a morale booster good food can be. I'm impressed by the way meals are served, too. The buffet tables could be catering a convention. No cheap serving bowls are seen here. Instead, large chafing dishes keep the food warm, and it is served in an orderly, welcoming manner.

In contrast to the outside of the Cajundome, people inside are in motion everywhere, everywhere except for the occasional sleeping body on a cot that might be next to a table registering people and giving out ID tags. Such contrasts are jolting and unpleasant. I sometimes feel as if I've stumbled into a place so private that I shouldn't be allowed in. Then a loud speaker comes on with an announcement that children not yet placed in schools are being registered on the second floor. It's surreal. Nothing fits together in the usual manner. If I find it slightly nightmarish, what must it feel like to those who have nowhere else to go?

The line for new volunteers to get ID passes is long, even this late in the game. The process involves turning over the information from your driver's license, having your picture taken, and printing out a laminated ID with a clip to attach it to your shirt. Some of the people handling the new volunteers are pretty new themselves. They are just learning the game and stumble somewhat. They are watched over by an official Red Cross person who makes them even more nervous and stumbling. Residents seem to be getting their ID passes at the same desk.

Sunday, September 18

The responses to my e-mail requests are proving to be overwhelming. I haven't received a formal accounting of how much support has been raised by this simple appeal, but I have been told that the Louisiana Association for the Education of Homeless Children and Youth is astonished at the extent of its reach. Contributions are coming from across the country in amounts that make it possible to provide for hundreds of students who literally left everything behind. In addition to gifts of money, some NWP sites sent goods. Diane Penrod at Rowan University galvanized an amazing effort among the New Jersey sites that included, along with personal checks, fleece-lined jackets, book bags, school supplies, computers, even teddy bears. She sent eight boxes, each weighing more than fifty pounds. I was not surprised. I knew my teacher friends would reach out to help the children.

And as for my request for items of basic hygiene for the men outside the shelters, it took more than four hours to package all the little bottles and other items that came from NWP colleagues. In the end, each jumbo baggie held a wash cloth, soap, toothpaste and toothbrush, deodorant, shaving cream, razors, a comb, Band-Aids, nail clippers or a file, and a small mirror, along with at least one little bottle of shampoo. The baggies filled four oversized boxes.

Jayne Marlink and her California NWPers went one step beyond. They packed their own health kits and mailed them to a church distribution center. The church received so many boxes that the priest called to ask me if I could tell him who or what the California Writing Project is. I did, or tried to.

Tuesday, September 20

It is interesting that Greg Davis refers to the evacuees as "guests." It neatly sums up his attitude towards them. He is their advocate and defender. I admire him for being able to imagine how it would feel to be on the receiving end of this effort.

Wednesday, September 21

Last night provided a prime example of the staff's concern for the well-being of the residents. With Hurricane Rita eerily imitating Katrina, they decided they should have an evacuation drill in case they have to get the residents out of here en route to a safer shelter. I didn't know it, but because the Cajundome was not built to withstand major hurricane-force storms, it can be used as a shelter only after a storm, not as an evacuation center during a hurricane. And now it looks as if there is a good possibility of a major hurricane coming our way—again.

I wasn't there to see it, but by all accounts it was masterful. Phil Ashurst was at it again, planning and replanning how to get people out in an orderly, safe manner. If the time comes to put the plan into operation for real, they will know what to do. I wish the television cameras that showed the disorder of the Louisiana Superdome were here to show what is being done right.

Thursday, September 22

Hurricane Rita is approaching the coast. Last night it seemed headed to Galveston, but this morning it has taken a turn to the north, and Louisiana is threatened once again. Thank goodness the Cajundome staff took the residents through an evacuation drill a couple of nights ago because the building is not structurally sound enough to withstand a Category 4 or 5 hurricane. Now it looks as if the drill will turn into the real thing.

The staff has been in meetings all morning. Despite yesterday's announcement that the Cajundome will not be evacuated, rumors are running everywhere that the plan has changed. The atmosphere is charged as people run from one office to another. I've heard that the buses are set to arrive at 3 P.M. to take people to Shreveport. They will return after the storm—if the Cajundome is in shape to receive them.

Greg Davis is talking with the Shreveport people to make sure that the residents will be treated well. He is concerned that they won't receive the kind of care they have been given here. I can hear him on the phone with people at the CenturyTel Center, stressing the fact that they have already been through so much that they need to be treated generously and hospitably. Pat Wright, Davis' executive secretary, is in charge of getting people on the buses. The anxiety level rises with each weather update. Yesterday the cone predicting the hurricane's path barely touched Louisiana; today it covers the entire coast. FEMA is leaving and going to Cameron Parish. Why? One of the young women with FEMA is in tears, frightened in the face of Rita. All she knows about hurricanes is what she has seen on TV from Katrina.

You couldn't write a movie this bad.

Monday, September 26

It happened. Rita hit southwest Louisiana long and hard on the twenty-third, right along the Texas-Louisiana border. Power is still out in some places, and just west of Lafayette there was serious flooding, fallen trees, and downed power lines. Déjà vu. There will be more evacuees. As someone said, "Hit the reset button."

The Cajundome took some water during Rita, but as of noon today everything will be fixed except some glass at the top that can wait. Ceiling tiles have been replaced. In the meantime, help continues to come in from unsolicited sources. If the ones I happen to know about are like other institutions and organizations that I don't know about, this is an incredibly generous country. For example, the New York City Writing Project collected books for displaced teachers. Under the leadership of Felicia George and Linette Moorman and with the help of Jane Haspel, former director of the Greater New Orleans Writing Project, and Elaine White, director of the Live Oak Writing Project in Mississippi, NYC Teacher Consultants spent a Saturday in December wrapping the books and writing individual letters to the teachers who were to receive them. Some who could not be there donated additional books or money for the project. As White wrote in return, "We gathered our teacher consultants this past Saturday for an SOS (Saturday Outreach Session). It was our first meeting since Hurricane Katrina. I wish you could have seen the expressions on the faces of our group as we directed them to the stacks of books your site sent. It was like Christmas!"

One of the most creative means of raising funds for

hurricane relief was a standard NWP event: the Writing Marathon. Tish McGonegal and her Vermonters, Tanya Baker in Maine, Faye Gage at the Connecticut Writing Project–Fairfield, Marjorie Roemer at the Rhode Island Writing Project, and other site directors asked participants to make a donation to participate, then sent the gifts to their Louisiana colleagues. Richard Louth of Southeastern Louisiana University received a check for $250 raised by a writing marathon sponsored by the Secangu Writing and Action Project in Mission, South Dakota. The site director, Sherry Red Owl Neiss, asked that it be used to help children of the Houma Indian nation. The Philadelphia Writing Project continues to send support raised by its relief projects. All these efforts are appreciated, and all donations gratefully received.

I think I'm dreaming all this. It couldn't be real.

Tuesday, September 27

The Cajundome, which had worked its way from crisis mode at the outset of Katrina relief to a maintenance mode, is back to crisis. I guess you could call it feverish preparation mode. Yesterday the staff put out cots and tried to get ready for the new and returning evacuees. Today buses are on the way, and there is once again the need to register people, get them settled, feed them, and give them water. The walkie-talkies are sending and receiving, trying to get supplies unloaded and people tended to. There is haste and bustle. Adrenaline is flowing. Security has put the Cajundome on lockdown in anticipation of arrivals.

Later in the day, evacuees have arrived and continue to arrive from Vermilion and Cameron parishes. There are 1,200 people in the Convention Center now. Unlike before, many people just walked up to the shelter, and lots drove in. A couple of buses arrived. One of them has been waiting outside for quite some time. I don't know how long. Greg Davis says to expect around four thousand new evacuees. He has gone on local television station KATC to put out a call for volunteers.

The evacuees to Shreveport have not yet returned, but they will soon. Then what will happen? How will stressed-out strangers who have lost so much react to each other? There is talk of a culture clash: How will the poor, urban, mostly black residents from New Orleans and the poor, rural, mostly white evacuees from the southwestern part of the state get along? It's pretty close quarters around here, and to share it with people you don't know and who aren't like you could be dicey.

President Bush is meeting with Homeland Security's emergency operations center in Lake Charles today.

Wednesday, September 28

Preparations continue even as new evacuees arrive. Today there is to be a planning session to get ready for the returning residents, who are scheduled to get "home" around 3 P.M. The Cajundome staff wants to minimize any potential conflict among the two resident groups and allay any discontent the returning residents may feel in the face of changes that have taken place while they were gone. In an effort to make the environment as congenial and comfortable as possible, staff members are talking about doing a number of things, including wearing matching shirts to identify staff members and devising a long-range strategy, since it is anticipated that the residents will be here for five weeks. In addition, they are trying to reestablish services, such as on-site after-school tutoring, an off-site transitional school, and recreational programs including physical activities such as flag football, as well as video games, televisions, card games, and bingo. They want to create an attractive and entertaining environment to minimize "cultural clash."

Chef Gilbert is preparing a special meal to welcome everyone back tomorrow night. The Shreveport contingent was promised a celebration when they returned, and they're going to get it. Greg Davis is writing a letter to them to explain the changes and reorganization that have taken place since they left.

The number of new evacuees from Cameron and Vermilion is dropping off.

Thursday, September 29

Yesterday's careful planning fell victim to other people's negligence, at best, or manipulation, at worst. After the staff got the returned evacuees settled in late last night, another six buses arrived unexpected and unannounced at one in the morning. According to the evacuees from the Cameron-Vermilion area, who were being housed in Bossier City, and the bus drivers, they were told by a Red Cross official to board buses and their drivers were told to follow a police car to the CenturyTel Center. From there they were transferred to other buses with instructions to go to the Cajundome in Lafayette. No notice was given to the Cajundome, which, needless to say, was not ready for them. They were told that they either had to go to Lafayette or within twenty-four to thirty-six hours they would be sent further away from their homes, perhaps to Arkansas. They surmise that they were being kicked out because of a hockey game. Greg Davis is very angry. He even went on TV to tell the story and assign blame to the uncaring, unfeeling people who would dump homeless, desperate people on someone else with no notice—all for a hockey game.

Gov. Kathleen Blanco called. She wanted to know what was going on, and a member of her staff is looking into the situation.

Saturday, October 1

The district fire marshal and his aides are here today looking into the crowding. It is a problem, but what can anyone do? The fire officials are requiring that exits remain as clear as possible and traffic lanes stay open, while the staff, Red Cross, and volunteers still try to treat people humanely. They are not doing an official fire watch, but simply observing. They are wearing brown today, rather than white, in an effort to be low-key. They mentioned that they are not barking orders, but making requests. Obviously they are sympathetic to people's feelings and fears.

Apparently people are still leaving their homes in Calcasieu, Cameron, and Vermilion parishes as they realize the situation there isn't getting better. The fire marshal suggests taking in people who just show up but not making an announcement that the Cajundome is open for more people. It is close to full.

The missing link in all this puzzle is the temporary housing that is supposed to materialize. Apparently there is none available in Lafayette Parish. There is nowhere for people to go. In the meantime, everyone here is getting the best treatment that can be provided.

One Red Cross official has called it "the Hilton of shelters." He went on to say that if his home in North Carolina is ever damaged, he's coming here. Actually, I think there has been some disagreement between Red Cross people and the Cajundome staff about the quality of the food and lodgings. The Red Cross maintains that if the "refugees" continue to be so well treated they won't want to leave. I can't believe that. No matter how well fed and entertained people are, everyone wants to go home. Everyone wants be in his own home, around his own friends and neighbors.

CHAPTER 9

The Relief Stories

The Shreveport Story
Source: *James Bloom*

With Rita growing larger and closer with each passing hour, the Cajundome staff realized that their residents would have to be evacuees a second time. The shelter could not withstand a storm the size of Rita. They would have to be moved—again. This time, the staff resolved, the move might be upsetting, but it would be orderly and safe.

Getting ready for a possible exodus, but still hoping it wouldn't be necessary, the staff conducted a rehearsal two nights before everyone had to leave. When the time came, the residents knew where to assemble, what they could take, which bus to board, and where their belongings would be stored in their absence. They executed the drill like well-trained troops, moving smoothly in sections from the bleachers to the buses that would take them to yet another shelter, this time in Shreveport.

The arrival was to be less comfortable than the departure. When the evacuees were dropped off at

Southern University at Shreveport, they were met by Army Reserve personnel pointing automatic weapons at them. "Why do you think you need weapons," they asked. "We're no harm to anyone." The armed men replied that they had no control of the policy. "The Red Cross is in charge," they said. "It's out of the university's hands."

The experience was not to get better. One of the Cajundome residents said they were "treated like dirt and common criminals. When they fed us, they fed us out of ice chests. For each meal the female Red Cross workers that were in charge said 'those people' were hiding food to eat later on. When I tried to explain to them that the kids were getting food for the elderly, handicapped, and little kids so that they would not have to stand in line, they replied that they were in charge and no one could have five plates at a time. Everyone had to get in line whether they were old or young."

On Saturday morning James Bloom, an evacuee who was a graduate of the Southern University system, spoke with Chancellor Roy Belton, pointing out that the evacuees were hurt by the way the Red Cross was treating them. In response he received only an explanation that "the situation was out of his control." Bloom replied, "Thank you, brother, but if Dr. Bash were at SUNO or Dr. Jesse Stone [former administrators], they would never treat our people this way."

The evacuees reported that three different Red Cross workers announced that the residents were returning home, but each time they were wrong, leaving the double evacuees with dashed hopes. As Bloom said,

"Keep in mind that we were of all colors and from all nations, and former chancellors would never have allowed the Red Cross to treat us as they did."

Bridging Religious Differences
Source: Pam DeVille

In the early days of the Cajundome shelter, a well-dressed family of three appeared seeking shelter. They were apparently people of some means, surprised to find themselves in the shelter. Their cultural traditions seemed to set them apart from the other evacuees. The Cajundome staff managed to find them another place to live, but the father complained of the food. "It isn't kosher," he said.

Hearing his comment, the staff assumed the family was Jewish and placed a call to Temple Shalom asking for help. Dr. Edye Mayers, a member of the temple, knew of a house in Breaux Bridge that was owned by a New Yorker who used it only when he wanted to spend a weekend dancing to Zydeco music. She got in touch with him and secured the house for the family—free of charge for two months.

Only after all the negotiations had been completed did the staff learn that the family was not Jewish. They were Muslim. A flurry of calls ensued to renegotiate the agreement. The Jewish New Yorker remained true to his word and turned his house over to his Muslim tenants. A few weeks later he even came to visit just to make sure they were comfortable.

Getting Through the Red Tape
Source: Marlene Jarvis

This is the story of Marlene Jarvis, an evacuee from the Metairie area who had problems at every step of the process in trying to get assistance from the proper agencies. She was a young, white, single parent desperate to get her life in order so that she could resolve complicated family court issues involving custody of her young son. As she saw her situation, all the service agencies had failed her.

According to Jarvis, she applied for Red Cross aid several times, but every time she asked, they were out of the debit cards they had been distributing. Consequently, she was not approved for her Red Cross card, but could not find out where to go to file another application. As she reported it, even the information desk could not tell her how to proceed. She turned to the Salvation Army, but its spokesperson said it was not in a position to help.

She applied in person at FEMA, but was denied assistance on the basis of misinformation. Her FEMA records stated that she had no expenses for moving, did not hold a job at the time of the storm, and was Spanish speaking—all of which she maintained was incorrect.

At some point she must have received some funds from FEMA, because she reported that she used them as a down payment on an apartment. However, because of a long-standing electric bill that someone ran up under her name when she was a student at

ULL, her power could not be turned on unless she paid the old bill by the fifth of October. She had no furniture, and if she had to pay a deposit and the electric bill, she would not be able to buy any. The deeper significance of not being able to secure a place to live is that she could not get custody of her child until she had one. As she tried to work out the problems, she explained that she could not even talk to her son by telephone because her mother-in-law would not permit it. Everything had to be in place by the next day or she would lose her case for custody.

Jarvis has lupus, which is exacerbated by stress. At the time she told her story, she was close to hysterical, certainly angry, and desperate. I don't know what became of her.

He Fooled Everyone—Almost
Source: Pat Wright

Everyone says he was charming. Everyone fell for his story.

How could you not? He took the call in public. Standing at the front desk in the Cajundome administrative offices, he learned that he had lost his wife and children along with everything he had. His grief was passionate and public. He had nothing left, and all who heard his story felt sympathy for the loss he was trying to endure.

As the days wore on, the compassion of those around him took various forms. People had him in their homes for dinner. They gave him clothes and drove him where he wanted to go. He enjoyed Lafayette's restaurants through the hospitality of those who wanted to comfort him. They gave him haircuts, watches, and more. He was scheduled to spend the coming weekend with a Lafayette family at their camp.

He became so well-known around the Cajundome that eventually the press picked up his story. A reporter asked him to tell it once again so that she could record and publish it. He willingly told it once more, reveling in all the attention he was getting. The reporter, who noticed a discrepancy in the various versions of his tale, grew suspicious of its veracity. After the interview she ran a background check on him and found that he was wanted for rape in Dallas. He is now behind bars.

Remembrance
By John St. Julien

On my first day I helped a lady from St. Bernard Parish file for help from FEMA. She chatted amiably as I filled in her application online, a process which required that I ask about details of her life, including her finances, that I'm sure she would have rather kept private. She had lost everything she owned and knew she would not be able to return to her home or her job as a classroom aide for months or perhaps ever. I became acutely aware that she was exhibiting more grace and dignity in this terrible situation than I have ever possessed. She and I saw each other several more times over the next few weeks. She took a job cleaning hotels in New Orleans, even though she suffered from arthritis, riding back and forth every day on a bus that left before daylight and returned well after dark. On many days she missed supper because the bus returned too late. She was unable to find other housing and worried whether she would be able to find transportation to her job in New Orleans after the shelter closed. Despite all this, she remained gracious, courteous, and cordial. I will remember her and the way she conducted herself under conditions of incredible hardship.

The Lost Are Found
Source: Giselle Cormier

A father and daughter who had been separated twenty-four years earlier were, unknown to either of them, both evacuated to the Cajundome. The father was sleeping in the arena directly below the bed of his daughter on the level above. In the line for dinner one night he recognized his daughter's uncle—her mother's brother. The father spoke to him and discovered that his long-lost daughter was in the shelter, too. The reunion was a surprise and a joy.

The daughter has now gone back to New Orleans, but she and her father continue to keep in touch now that they have found each other. The father said, "And to think I've been looking for her for twenty-four years."

PART IV

The Relocation Phase

Home is the place where, when you have to go there, they have to take you in.
                                        —Robert Frost

CHAPTER 10

The Diaspora

After two weeks of living at the Cajundome, the residents displaced by Hurricane Rita were anxious to return home. However, because electricity had not yet been restored throughout the area and potable water was not available everywhere, the authorities could not arrange to send them back. The residents who had fled Katrina and the consequent flooding of Orleans, Jefferson, Plaquemines, and St. Bernard parishes had been at the Cajundome even longer. Frustration levels were high as FEMA workers and others struggled to find housing for those who had none and transportation for those who would eventually be allowed to return to their homes.

Family Net was one of the organizations formed to help people find somewhere to go. The chaotic exodus from New Orleans following Katrina, and sometimes the relief efforts themselves, parted family members, sometimes sending them to different parts of the country. Hotie Siebert, a woman who saw the need for a process by which families could be reunited, put out a call on KRVS radio for volunteers to help reunite families, and those who responded served effectively throughout the Relief Phase to assist evacuees who were desperately seeking to find loved ones, hoping they were still alive. The volunteers did not necessarily know each other; they just started working together to help families get back together.

Some of the people who turned to Family Net for help came on their own; others were referred by Foundation for Hope or the American Red Cross. The process was simple. Evacuees submitted the name and contact information of someone with whom they could live, and Family Net contacted that person to verify that it was a safe place for the evacuee to move. After the destination was approved, the organization sent the evacuee there by Greyhound bus or, for shorter trips, by personal driver.

Although no hard numbers are available, the loosely organized group managed to reunite a large number of people. Yet it was chronically hampered by lack of funding, as it was dependent on private donations for support. Siebert appealed to Angel Flight, a nonprofit organization that provides free air transportation for people in need, to assist with disabled or hardship cases and to the Red Cross for direct funding.

Evacuees arrived and departed throughout the fifty-eight days of the Cajundome shelter, but the diaspora took a serious leap forward over the weekend of October 1, when someone managed to get through to the Red Cross's toll-free number, a line that had been continually tied up. Once the connection was made, dozens of residents were eager to use it to file their claims and have their relief money sent to their home addresses. Doing so meant that they no longer had to be at the Cajundome to get their checks. They could leave. And they did.

On October 10, the pace quickened considerably. President Bush announced an October 15 deadline for emptying all shelters, and the Cajundome still had almost seven hundred residents. The goal was to reduce the number of residents to two hundred by October 15, but authorities were not yet letting buses into Lake Charles. Over the weekend FEMA surveyed residents regarding their housing needs and their willingness to relocate. Using that information, representative Tricia Schaefer, with Cajundome staff members Pam DeVille and Heidi Champagne and the Foundation for Hope, worked to move individuals and families into housing outside the Cajundome. The task was often frustrating due to communities' objections to FEMA trailer compounds, complicated family relationships, and lack of money. A telephone conversation overheard by bystanders in the Cajundome offices illustrated the problems involved in something as simple as arranging a return to the family home. A man in his mid-forties speaking with his mother made it clear that "going home" was no simple matter. "I know, Ma," he said. "I don't want to come either, but they say I got to get out of here, and I don't got no place else to go. . . . I know, Ma. I wish I didn't have to come either. I know. I know."

On October 12, two buses departed from the Cajundome to return people to their homes in Lake Charles and nearby towns. The move required an enormous effort on the part of many people to get everything arranged since each person had to have a verified place to stay, either his or her own home that had been inspected and approved or confirmation from a host who would take the person. Some people simply did not show up. At least twelve people who had filed applications to relocate disappeared, and nobody knew where they went.

In the final days of the relocation phase, FEMA worker Tricia Schaefer worked tirelessly to find land for mobile homes and provide transportation for people who had somewhere to go. She had come to the Cajundome early, arriving on September 1, the day fifty buses arrived with evacuees. Since that day she had done whatever needed to be done. She registered people so they could get help and scheduled buses for people to get to the disaster center to inquire about their claims. When evacuees couldn't get through to FEMA's toll-free telephone number, she called in an inspector to cut through the red tape. The work never ended. In one forty-hour period, Schaefer worked thirty-five hours. Officially she was responsible for Evangeline, Acadia, Lafayette, and St. Landry parishes, and personnel were stretched to an impossible point because the need was so widespread. As a result she had her own frustrations and the public's criticism.

Schaefer's own personal situation was not a simple one. She was deployed by FEMA immediately after Hurricane Katrina hit, which meant leaving her regular job without any assurance that it would be there for her when she returned. Unlike National Guard personnel, FEMA workers can be called up for an indefinite period, but their main jobs are not guaranteed. Workers cannot be sure that they will be able to return to their regular employment once their FEMA duties are completed. In addition, she missed her family, especially her granddaughter. Nevertheless, she stayed and worked because she was moved by the tragic plight of so many people. As she said, "The people mean more to me than all the political picture. Seeing people from the Vermilion and Cameron buses get off was heartbreaking."

In the relocation phase, Schaefer's days were long and intense. Working as long as she could keep going, she feverishly made arrangements for placing families throughout Acadiana and the rest of the country. She was a remarkable contrast to the image most Americans had formed about FEMA, though few heard of her or saw what she accomplished.

By Thursday, October 13, the number of residents had been sufficiently reduced for the staff to require everyone to move to the Convention Center in preparation for shutting down the Cajundome as a shelter. On that same day New Orleans mayor Ray Nagin visited the Cajundome, where he spoke with the residents, inviting, even urging them to return to the city. Calcasieu Parish announced that everyone could return there as well. Suddenly the shelter was closing down. After fifty-eight days of frenetic activity, the big halls and arena were growing empty.

A few residents would remain in the Convention Center for another week, but the Cajundome itself could now return to its original use. It would once again be an arena where people could enjoy sports and entertainment, and the fifty-eight days of cots and laundry, medical triage, food service for thousands, the information desk, the red vests of the Red Cross, and the orange T-shirts of the PRC, all of them would be memories.

In its fifty-eight days of serving as a shelter, the Cajundome had cared for some 18,500 evacuees, the average daily attendance fluctuating between 5,000 and 7,000 people the first few weeks and tapering off to an average of 1,200 in the last couple of weeks. The total number of evacuee days came to 102,663. It also provided sleeping quarters for several military units

including the 82nd Airborne from Fort Bragg, North
Carolina, and other Army units from Ft. Hood, Texas.
Some of the American Red Cross workers, medical
volunteers, and National Guard soldiers who were
assigned to work at the shelter also took residence
there. They averaged around thirty per night, as
many of them had off-site sleeping arrangements.

In that time the Cajundome served 362,300 meals
inside its walls, and another 43,700 off site at smaller
shelters. With a staff of seven, plus some part-time
workers and volunteers, they served more than four
hundred thousand meals at an amazing cost of $1.64
per meal. In contrast, the other staggering figure was
the total sheltering and recovery costs, which came to
$6.2 million.

At the peak of the evacuation, the American Red
Cross, which was officially in charge of running the
shelter, had 165 volunteers, with more than 600 people total offering their time over the fifty-eight days.
In actuality, the Red Cross worked in conjunction
with the Cajundome staff to provide adequate sleeping, eating, and sanitation conditions for the residents. Food, clothes, and other supplies came from
both the Acadiana area stores and individuals and
from the Red Cross, which drew goods from its four-
hundred-thousand-square-foot   warehouse   on
Highway 90 near Broussard. Their vehicles made two
runs a day between the Cajundome and the supply
center.

The Red Cross did not survive the situation without criticism. Because of its long experience in dealing with disasters, it has developed certain policies
that are to be enforced in any shelter that it runs. In
the case of the Cajundome, some of those rules and

regulations had to be relaxed for the welfare of the clients, such as a handwritten registration process that was slow and frustrating. The magnitude and complexity of the situation meant that what was done in the past was not always a suitable response to the Katrina and Rita disasters, and it became evident that the Red Cross needs to rewrite some of its protocols.

CHAPTER 11

A Reporter's Notebook

Monday, October 3

Over the weekend there was a large exodus of residents. Someone got through to the Red Cross on its toll-free number that has been generally inaccessible, and instead of hanging up when he was finished, he passed the telephone from one person to another. The line was open from seven o'clock one night until three o'clock the next afternoon. Once a person files his or her claim, Western Union can wire the money to any address given. In other words, an evacuee doesn't have to be at the Cajundome to get the money. Consequently, once people filed claims, they were free to leave. So much for not wanting to go home.

Today a couple of additional medical teams arrived, one with supplies.

Thursday, October 6

A host of small problems surfaced today—a stolen suitcase, ongoing medical problems, and such. Other than dealing with those, however, the Cajundome seems to be returning to maintenance mode. Things are settling back to the way they were before Katrina. Now there is much to do, but nothing like the crisis planning and management that I saw as Rita approached.

Dr. Paul Azar continues to come by to see about patients. He was remarkably well prepared for what he has done, given his military experience with MASH units. He has put together a PowerPoint presentation of both hurricanes and their aftermath, which is full of wonderful photographs. He has also kept a careful timeline.

Friday, October 7

Today is the birthday of a four-year-old boy living in the Cajundome. Deputy Kip Judice has left to go to Albertson's to buy a birthday cake and has put everybody on alert that when he brings the little boy in, everyone is to sing "Happy Birthday." He is looking for a toy to give him as a present, too. The sheriff's deputy is making a birthday party for a four year old.

Saturday, October 8

I took the story I wrote of Donald Williams and his group to them this morning. Donald wasn't there, but most of the rest of his "family" were. I offered it to Jared, but he said it looked long and he didn't read very fast. Yvonne began reading it, but immediately called Donald from her cell phone and asked him to return. He showed up quickly and took over the manuscript. He read to himself for a few minutes, then told the group that everyone should hear it. After getting everyone in a circle, he handed me the papers and asked me to read it. The group gave me rapt attention, reminding me of school children enthralled by their favorite story. They laughed at a few places, and when it was over, they had tears in their eyes. Even Donald was wiping tears from his cheeks. They were famous. People would know their story.

Sunday, October 9

The evacuees from Lake Charles are restless, anxious to return to their homes. The Cajundome staff is trying to arrange for buses to get them out. Part of the problem is that the authorities are not letting buses into Lake Charles yet. Tricia Schaefer, with FEMA at the Cajundome, is working with FEMA reps there to see if they can get at least one bus in. Electricity and potable water are not available throughout the city yet.

The atmosphere is crackling here. People are meeting, scurrying, making decisions behind closed doors. FEMA and others are stepping up the effort to get everyone's claims filed. I guess it's all about the need to get people out. The rumor is that they will close the Cajundome by October 15, but it hasn't been announced yet.

Thursday, October 13

I arrived late this morning and missed Mayor Nagin's speech to the residents. Everyone has a different opinion about it. The white residents charge that he wouldn't listen to them, only to the African-American evacuees. Some of the volunteers are outraged at what he promised the New Orleanians if they will return, claiming that it was totally unrealistic. He announced that anyone who had a small piece of dry land would receive a trailer, and he boasted of prosperous times for the city in the near future. According to this depiction, Katrina was a minor setback in the growth and development of New Orleans. I'm sorry I didn't get to see the show, but I didn't realize he was going to be here. I'm not sure if anyone did.

Monday, October 17

The numbers are still dropping. Security has been reduced. Everything seems strangely quiet and empty.

Wednesday, October 19

The last residents of the Cajundome shelter were moved today to the Domingue Recreation Center, a new facility near Comeaux High School in Lafayette. The event is over. All that remains is making a recovery—physical, financial, and emotional.

CHAPTER 12

The Relocation Stories

Villains and Heroes
By Audrey Leonard, as told by Greg Davis

Belden and Leah Chavis, an evacuated couple with twelve children, including two sets of twins, found themselves living in one room at the Hampton Inn in Lafayette. As they were required to pay each day in advance, they were soon down to their last forty dollars. Greg Davis, executive director of the Cajundome, reached in his pocket and gave the woman one thousand dollars and his cell-phone number. He told her to pay a week in advance. At least they would know they had a place to stay for the next week.

Leah called back later to tell Davis that the Hampton Inn would not take the money, and they had to get out. Davis got in touch with the Pastor's Resource Council, and the family was in a house of their own within twenty-four hours. No red tape.

Finding Families and Houses
Source: Michelle Wright

The pastor of a church in Raleigh-Durham, North

Carolina, called to check on the safety of a Cajundome resident named Siona Berard, a young woman who had been adopted by his church years ago. Although they had been estranged for some time, he still served as her guardian and felt an obligation to offer her help if she needed it. A few days later he arrived in Lafayette to make arrangements for her and her family to move to North Carolina. People in Raleigh-Durham had donated houses that they could use for up to a year. When he arrived, he also arranged to get them clothes, but for some reason the family decided not to go.

Volunteer Michelle Wright went to the Cajundome at 7:00 A.M. to try to find someone to take their place. She found a family, but the grandmother wouldn't go because her foster child had not been found. The two brothers-in-law decided that they would go to Raleigh-Durham with the preacher, and when they found the foster child, the rest would come. When the two men arrived there, they called back to report that everything was wonderful. Because their house wasn't quite ready, the church had put them up in the Hilton for a few days.

The remaining group was encouraged to get on their way. They had one car and lots of people. Six could go at a time—if the car would run. Unfortunately, the car had been broken into after the storm and the drive shaft had been damaged, so they had hot wired it to get to Lafayette. It was not ready for the long trip to Raleigh-Durham. Wright talked to the local Lincoln-Mercury dealership, Courtesy Lincoln-Mercury, who said they would send a wrecker, but they advised her that repairing the drive shaft would be expensive. To everyone's surprise, the Lincoln-Mercury service department called the next day to say that the car was ready to go, and there was no charge. Then Saturn of Lafayette paid for it to be realigned. The first group left in the repaired car at 5 P.M. for Raleigh-Durham, with the rest of the family to fly out on Saturday, using tickets Wright had bought for them.

The family planned to meet and have lunch before catching the plane, but when they got together, it turned out that the mother had disappeared. In the end, only four of the five plane tickets were used, but the Continental agent took care of the nonrefundable tickets by pushing them back for later use.

The final contingent left at last on September 28, making them a group of eight who took the house in Raleigh-Durham originally donated to another evacuee. It was not long before they had found jobs there.

Going to Orlando
Source: *Charles Doucet*

"They say they have an apartment for me in Orlando, just for me. Is that true?" he asked. "They say they'll help me find a job, too, and buy me a ticket to get there. Do you think that's so?" Charles Doucet's life had held little but pain and loss over the past three weeks, and he found it hard to believe something so good had come his way.

Doucet had lived in Lake Charles for five years when Hurricane Rita destroyed his home. Trained in a culinary school in San Francisco, he had lived on the West Coast for several years. He had recently decided to return to Louisiana because, he explained, it was time to "begin living life on my terms." At the time of the storm he was working as a chef, cooking offshore for British Petroleum.

On the Friday before Rita hit the Lake Charles area, Doucet, alarmed at the track the storm was taking, called his wife urging her to leave and go to Shreveport ahead of him. He promised to join her as soon as he could, but when he got home on Saturday morning she was still there, waiting for him. By then it was too late for anybody to leave. Rita had arrived. They would ride the storm out together.

As Rita's fury intensified, the two of them lay together in their bed trying to sleep. The trees outside lashed the house, as the gusting winds whipped their branches from side to side. Then a large oak tree in the back yard fell victim to the storm and crashed into the house. Coming through the roof, it fell directly on their bed, trapping Charles's wife beneath it. Two weeks later his hands still showed the marks of the wounds he incurred trying to move the tree and free her. He performed CPR on her, and when the eye of the hurricane rolled over Lake Charles, he picked her up and ran the two blocks to the hospital. The hospital staff told him that she died when the tree hit her.

Doucet had buried his wife the week prior, and his grief remained deep and painful. His children came from San Francisco and urged him to return with them, but he was not ready to leave her. For seven days he stayed as close to her in death as he could, sleeping on her grave in the cemetery. He could not eat. He could not leave. He could only grieve and pray.

He still deeply mourned his loss. She continued to be his role model, his inspiration, and nothing and no one could take her place. Before her death, when he did bad things, she would pray for him, he said. He would try to shut out her prayers with the TV, but he couldn't stop her from caring for him. After death, she continued to influence his behavior. Despite his grief, he had not taken a drink or turned to drugs because he knew she would not have wanted him to. Even his children could not give him solace. To deal with this, he said, "I simply need some time for myself."

Small slivers of hope began to appear alongside his grief. He began to trust the Foundation for Hope, the agency that made the promises of an apartment and a job, a new start in a place that had no sad memories. His eyes smiled when he talked about getting a job and taking charge of his life again. "If I can work," he said, "I'll be O. K."

This is the story as he told it. It turned out to be completely false, except that he did go to Orlando. His listeners had been so moved by the story that they had forgotten that no fatalities occurred in Lake Charles from Rita. When he returned to tell his story again the next day, embellished with new details, awareness dawned on his audience. He was a performer, not a grieving husband.

Edward and Michael
Source: Edward and Michael Gonzales

Edward and Michael Gonzales are brothers who used to live in New Orleans. They were on their way to Ohio, which to them could just as well be Timbuktu. They had never been there and weren't really sure where it was. They followed their mother from office to office as she negotiated for an apartment on her cell phone, then waited for a fax to confirm the arrangements. They moved listlessly, purposelessly behind her, waiting for their lives to change in yet another unknown and unexpected way.

Edward was fourteen and was in the ninth grade the last time he went to school. He wore baggy jeans that sagged around his knees and ankles. His head was wrapped with a bandana tied in a knot in the back, and his knit shirt with an alligator logo was several sizes too large—just the way he wanted it. He listened to rap music through earphones, bobbing his head to a silent rhythm. He was tall and thin, polite, quiet, undirected. He hadn't seen the inside of a classroom for six weeks, just the Cajundome and the part of it he shared with his brother and mother.

Michael was twelve, somewhat small for his age, with large round eyes that seldom blinked. His speech was difficult to understand, partly because of the heavy accent he carried from the Eighth Ward of New Orleans and partly from shyness that made him mumble. He wore a small plastic fan on a red cord around his neck. When it had batteries he could click a button and fan himself.

Edward and Michael had left New Orleans with their mother in their auntie's car before Katrina made landfall six weeks ago. They had been in shelters ever since. They were first sent to a church on Stone Avenue in Lafayette, then to the Cajundome, their "home" for more than a month. When asked how they spend their days, Edward said he talked on his cell phone to friends scattered to Houston and Dallas. He used the computers in the computer room and had some books to read. "The food be all right some-times," he said. Once in a while they even served pizza, his favorite. Michael, a seventh grader, liked sports, especially basketball and football, but he missed the opportunities to play at the Cajundome. Twice he managed to go to college games at the Ragin' Cajun stadium. He said they were good. Actually, Michael liked to play all kinds of games, and he spent some of his time playing games on the computers at the Cajundome. The rest of the day, he said, "I walks around the building, then goes back to my sleeping area." He had read no books since arriving there, but he had made some new friends over the past several weeks, and they went to "the courts" together.

Edward and Michael agreed that the hardest part of being in the shelter was putting up with the noise people made. It kept them awake at night. They said they had not been afraid, but they didn't like the commotion.

They were moving to Ohio now. As soon as the final details were arranged, they would board a Greyhound headed to their new lives. Their cousin lived there, and they looked forward to going back to school. It had been a long hiatus, and they were ready to begin whatever came next.

Joanne's Story
By Joanne Reeves

I really didn't get a chance to mingle with the residents very much, because my job was to answer the phone and take care of the front lobby. However, I did get a chance to see joy on the residents' faces when they would come in to use the phone to call a family member or when they found out that they had a place to go. The majority of my calls were from family members looking for other family members that they heard might be at the Cajundome. I would write down the names of the people calling, their numbers, and the names of the people they were looking for and turn them over to the Red Cross and let them do the paging. I really never found out if contact was made, but I did get a few calls back telling me thank you. When I would get those calls, it would make me feel like I had done something good.

As the weeks went by, I could see that most of the residents were ready to get their own place. FEMA was here and working as fast as it could. Residents were coming in wanting to talk to them; I tried to help them as much as I could. Some of them were O. K. with the answers I gave them, and of course, some were not. Some people felt I should know more. That was when Tricia Schaeffer or Kathy Bark with FEMA would come out and basically tell them the same thing that I had just said. Trailers were not coming in fast enough. Residents were getting frustrated. They wanted answers!! That was when I would get an earful from them.

During that time, there was one resident who would come in just to check on me, he would say. He would just open the door and say hi. Courtlander Collins was his name; he was a disabled single person. He would be placed in a trailer when they came in. Everyday he would come by and ask if his name was still on the list, say hi, and check on me. Then one day Tricia came in and told me that she had a travel trailer ready and she would place Courtlander. I was so happy for him! He came in as usual to tell me hi and showed me his new coat that he had just received. He said to me, "Ms. Joanne, look at what a lady just gave me. It is a little small, but it feels fine. I just know that today may be my lucky day." I wanted to tell him about the trailer, but I didn't just in case something went wrong.

He walked in later that day and told me that he heard his name had been called. All I could do was look at him and smile. He told me that he just knew I had something to do with his luck on this day, but really I didn't. It was the effort of Tricia with FEMA. Of course, I did ask every day if today was the day for Courtlander. He came in and sat by my desk with tears in his eyes and said he was leaving soon, that he had gotten a trailer. He called me just before Thanksgiving to see how I was doing. He was so happy to finally have a place of his own. I was touched by his patience and understanding. I realized how blessed I have been throughout this. I have a home, know where my family is, and am able to go to them everyday.

Living High in California
Source: Giselle Cormier

He was an unattractive man, scrawny and ill shaven, with eyes that never looked directly at you. He was deferential when asking for help, even a little obsequious. But that was when he was talking to people in authority. In conversation with fellow residents, he used his other moves to get money, drugs, and other life-enhancing items. His manipulation of people and the system was skillful. He was Mosca, Elmer Gantry, the flim-flam man, the con artist.

Enough became enough. The Cajundome staff decided he needed to move on and found him a room at a hotel in Newport Beach, California. The flim-flam man landed again in the chips. The room was at the Hyatt

Regency. Even with such an attractive destination, there were suspicions that he might not get there. He had missed other opportunities to leave; he might miss this one, too. To be sure he left, the sheriff's office notified him that two deputies would pick him up at 6:30 A.M. and personally put him on a plane to California.

To make sure he arrived at the Hyatt Regency, Giselle Cormier, business director for the Cajundome, called the hotel a few days later to check on him. Oh, yes, he had made it. The hotel reported that he had checked into a room provided for him rent free for a month and was making a regular routine of ordering drinks from the bar, movies from the front desk, and meals from the restaurant. The flim-flam man was in full operational mode. Again.

Starting Over
Source: Anthony Menard

Anthony Menard got out of New Orleans before the city was in trouble. Watching Katrina grow larger and closer to Louisiana every day, he boarded a Greyhound bus and headed out. He weathered the storm in a hotel room in a small town north of New Orleans. He was safe, but the money he had with him was dwindling.

After New Orleans fell into the chaos caused by the breeched levees, Menard became worried about his cousin, a relative he had not seen in a couple of years but who probably needed help since she had serious mental problems. He began to search online through www.locatelovedones.com and found her at the Cajundome. By the time he reached her, she had been at the shelter for a month.

Menard is a native of Washington, D. C., where he attended culinary school. He moved to New Orleans seven years ago to cook at Red Fish Grill, the Court of Two Sisters, Westin Hotel, and other restaurants in the French Quarter. He reasoned that there was little for him to return to, at least now, so he headed for D. C. again, taking his cousin with him. He found a two-bedroom apartment that would accommodate them, and he was confident that he could find a job. It was a thirty-hour bus ride, but Menard said he did not like airplanes. "People weren't meant to fly," he said.

He shook his head when he talked of what happened to New Orleans after Katrina. "My people," he said, "are the only people who kill and hurt their own." Something like anger blazed up when he mentioned the big-screen televisions he saw people looting. "I would take food and water if my family needed it," he said, "but television sets. No way."

Menard grew impatient with his cousin, too. She seemed paralyzed, unable to make a decision. He had spent all he had trying to find her and help her, and she vacillated between staying and going. She didn't seem to realize that staying was not an option. He would go alone if in the end she would not leave, he said. His life had been on hold, but he was starting again. His eyes were bright with expectation. He wanted to get on that bus as soon as possible, find the apartment that had been promised him, put on his cook's uniform, and start making the rounds of the restaurants in Georgetown. Anthony Menard would be all right.

PART V

The Recovery Phase

A memory is what is left when something happens and does not completely unhappen.
—Edward de Bono

CHAPTER 13

Acadiana Regroups

Once the post-Katrina rescue and relief efforts were under control, city authorities, led by Lafayette city-parish president Joey Durel, turned their attention to the long-term impact of the storm on Lafayette. Recognizing that the greatest rebuilding project in U. S. history was about to begin, the task force had to make sure that Lafayette would not be left out. While it recognized the importance of finding a significant role for Lafayette to play in the reconstruction process, it did not want to appear to be greedy or predatory. The task force was also concerned about projections that Lafayette would achieve overnight the population growth that had been anticipated for 2020, making it necessary to draw up plans for this unnatural growth. Lafayette would immediately need a new elementary school, middle school, and high school. It would also need new roads.

These concerns led the task force to create guidelines for its actions. The plans include expanding on LINC (Lafayette in a New Century), a comprehensive plan for the area that had already been established; drawing up a federal wish list for the city, and doing everything possible to help businesses in the impacted areas reestablish themselves. Some businesses were flourishing as a result of Katrina and Rita, but others were struggling to survive because the evacuation efforts had shut them down. In addition, efforts were made to urge businesses not returning to New Orleans to stay in the state and encourage businesses that were returning to New Orleans to keep an office in Lafayette.

Durel was charged with taking the wish list to Washington, D. C. Realizing that some of the requests would be seen like "pork" and the city as avaricious, Durel in the end did not submit it to the senators and congressmen he visited. One item on the list was a monorail system connecting University Medical Center, the Cajundome/Convention Center, and the University of Louisiana at Lafayette at a cost of $50 million. Realizing that there was little chance of securing funding for such projects at that time, Durel, along with Lafayette civic leaders Kam Movassaghi and Daryl Byrd, decided to work not just for Lafayette, but for the state as a whole. They also lobbied legislators to include Lafayette in any economic incentive packages that became available.

Before Congress, Durel pledged that Lafayette would play a major role in the rebuilding of Louisiana. He argued that it is uniquely poised to do so, as it is located at the crossroads of I-49 and I-10, the center of technology in the state because of its fiber installation and the university's involvement in computer science, and the only major city in Louisiana that had showed growth over the past fifteen years due to expansion of business and industry.

Because Lafayette was affected by Katrina to roughly the same degree as Baton Rouge and affected by Rita more seriously than was Baton Rouge, making it the most affected city outside of the devastated areas, the group asked the legislators to support Lafayette's efforts to expand and strengthen its already strained infrastructure. Specifically, they urged Congress to complete I-49 from Lafayette to New Orleans, expand I-10 from Mississippi to Texas to six lanes, and help to make Lafayette a major staging area for the rebuilding effort. Durel stressed the importance of making sure that the money follows the people so that businesses can grow and thereby restore the state.

Durel pointed out that the Chinese define the word "chaos" as "opportunity." If that be so, it follows that all the dislocations, disruptions, and disturbances that Hurricanes Katrina and Rita had caused could, in the long run, create possibilities for the city's future that had not been available in the past. The storms had not changed Lafayette's destiny, he said. It was still destined for greatness; the only thing that was different was how it was going to happen. As the city and parish moved into the recovery phase, he and the task force focused on preparing for growth and development.

Equally concerned about the impact of the storms was one of the owners of the Cajundome, the University of Louisiana at Lafayette. Looking back at the work of the shelter's staff, university president Ray Authement had nothing but praise for the rescue and relief efforts of Greg Davis, Pam DeVille, and the rest of the staff. Authement reflected that by providing the kind of care they gave to the evacuees, they brought honor and prestige to the university. When the Cajundome Commission met in late November, Authement moved that a plaque commemorating the two-month effort and recognizing the exemplary work of the staff be placed in the foyer of the Cajundome.

Using the facility as a shelter had both positive and negative consequences for the university. On one hand, the Cajundome earned favorable national publicity for the quality of care it provided, which by extension reflected well on the university. Major television news organizations such as CBS and CNN covered the story of the Cajundome's efforts to provide assistance for evacuees with dignity and compassion, often noting its relationship to the university. It should be pointed out that the university also provided space on campus in Bancroft Dormitory, closed at that time for renovation, to house 140 medics, plus Entergy line workers and Tulane University medical personnel.

The negative impact of using a university facility as a shelter was primarily economic. Authement stated that the Cajundome would require all the city's $500,000 obligation and needed FEMA to cover other expenses. Adding to the economic problems was the fact that for several months the Cajundome was not available for several large shows that traditionally use its space. Events such as the Louisiana Gulf Coast Oil Exposition (LAGCOE) and the annual Tinsels and Treasures holiday market, as well as ULL events, had to be cancelled, thereby reducing expected revenue.

As for the Cajundome itself, the epicenter of the sheltering occupation, eight weeks of occupancy by thousands of people left it in serious need of cleaning, repair, and restoration. In early September, operations director Phil Ashurst began putting together a budget for what would need to be done after the evacuees had left. He also contacted the Centers for Disease Control and Prevention, the Department of Health and Hospitals, and the Department of Environmental Quality to be sure all official standards and requirements were met. He estimated that in two weeks as a shelter the Cajundome had put the equivalent of two and a half years of demand on the air-conditioning system and eleven years of wear on the bathroom facilities. Annual and semiannual cleaning had become daily and weekly routines. The facility would need painting, carpet replacement, and cleaning of the soft textile walls.

The staff wasted no time in beginning the clean up as soon as the last remaining residents were relocated in the Convention Center. On October 14, they started the first stage of the restoration—cleaning the place. The production/conversion/setup department began by picking up equipment like trash cans, tables, and chairs, and relocating it to the arena floor where it was inspected for damages, sorted, sanitized with a hospital-grade disinfectant, and then cleaned. The same crew also began gathering disaster supplies—MREs, cots, air mattresses, blankets, and water—and placing and wrapping them onto pallets, counting them and then storing them in the arena. These pallets were eventually moved to the Convention Center after all the residents left and the floors and walls in the exhibit halls were cleaned.

Every piece of equipment in the building that had come into contact or potential contact with residents or bedding was sanitized and cleaned, inventoried, and then returned to the proper storage area. Broken items were inventoried and put into a separate location in the arena for repair or documentation before disposal. All soft-surface furniture was brought to

Exhibit Hall B for storage until cleaned or replacement furniture could be purchased. This included all suite furniture that was not either wood or leather and could not be wiped down with disinfectants and cleaners. At the outset of the postshelter operation, Bill Blanchet, assistant director of finance and production for the Cajundome, speculated that cleaning, repair, and restoration could cost up to $1.5 million.

The plan was to store up to 150 pallets of supplies, including 2,000 cots, 953 air mattresses, 1,500 blankets, 21,000 MREs, and 28,000 individual servings of water. The projection at its closing as a shelter was that the Cajundome would reopen in December for fall graduation ceremonies of the university. In actuality, it reopened for regular business on January 6, 2006.

CHAPTER 14

A Reporter's Notebook

Friday, October 14

The great cleaning of the Cajundome has begun, but it will take more than soap, water, and a good mop to get this place back to normal. It will also take paint, carpet, and carpentry. Housing and feeding more than eighteen thousand people for fifty-eight days will age any building at a faster than normal clip.

What a strange feeling it is to wander through the hallways and bleachers now devoid of people. Here and there you see concessions areas torn down, and everywhere there is trash to be swept away. I lean over one of the upper ledges and look down to imagine the hordes of people who were so recently milling about, sleeping, talking, watching TV. Where are they now? Where are Edward and Michael Gonzales and their mother who were so frightened by the prospect of going to Ohio? Are the boys finally back in school? Is Charles Doucet still telling his fraudulent story about the fall of the oak tree that took his wife's life as they slept in their home in Lake Charles? Have the frightened children learned to trust again? Are they laughing again?

You can't put a figure on the human costs of coping with Katrina and Rita. We will be paying for them for years to come. In a few months the outside of the Cajundome will look much as it did before the two storms ripped through our world, but it will be a long, long time before the lives they touched will approach being the same on the inside. They cannot avoid having been scarred by the experience, but for a few weeks in the late summer of 2005, the Cajundome in Lafayette cared for the people who came to it for help. They were taken in as friends and treated with compassion. Their hurts were treated, and their needs were met as well as it was humanly possible to do so.

The emptiness is eerie. The silence is loud. The adrenaline is subsiding. The memories remain.

Index

Acadian Ambulance, 53, 70, 101

Acadiana Arts Council, 91

Acadiana chapter of the American Red Cross, 38

Acadiana Symphony Orchestra, 20, 90

Acadiana Symphony Orchestra Conservatory, 83

Acadiana Writing Project, 99

American Red Cross (ARC), 17-21, 27, 33-35, 37-40, 43-45, 58, 60, 65, 70, 76-78, 82-83, 87-89, 93, 96, 101-2, 104, 110-12, 114, 116, 124, 127-28, 131, 142

Americares, 90

Aranza, Jacob, 47

Artisan Catering, 20

Ashurst, Phil, 18, 31-32, 76, 87, 105, 152

Authement, Ray, 151-52

Azar, Paul, 44, 76, 132

Baker, Tanya, 108

Baptist Men of Texas, 35

Bartlett, Keith, 90

Barton, Clara, 37

Begnaud, Cyd, 45

Bell South, 36, 77

Benoit, Gene, 36

Bishop, Sharon, 59

Blanchet, Bill, 34-35, 75, 154

Blanco, Kathleen, 111

Blaylock, Andy, 45

Brothers, Colleen, 70

Brown, Shirley, 59

"Bubba crews," 19, 35

Burton, Shanna, 36

Byrd, Daryl, 150

Cajun Field, 20, 102

Cajundome, 22

Carter, Mark, 49

Centennial Wireless, 77

Centers for Disease Control and Prevention, 82, 152

CenturyTel Center, 21, 106, 110

Chamber of Commerce, 80, 91

Champagne, Heidi, 76, 125

Children's Museum of Acadiana, 91

Cingular, 77-78, 96

Cisco Systems, 78

city marshal, 51
city-parish government, 76, 93
Clark, Ron, 46
Coast Guard, 69
College of Nursing and Allied Health Professions, 92
Comeaux Recreation Center, 22
Connecticut Writing Project—Fairfield, 108
Cormier, Giselle, 119, 143-44
Cox Communications, 77, 96
Credeur, Tony, 19, 38

Daily Advertiser, The, 39-40
Davis, Greg, 17, 20, 34, 39-40, 47, 61, 64, 71, 82, 100, 105-6, 109-11, 135, 151
Day, Stephanie, 45
DeCourt, Gilbert, 81
Department of Environmental Quality, 153
Department of Health and Hospitals, 153
Department of Homeland Security, 41, 51, 53, 109
Department of Labor and Job Services, 77, 98
Department of Motor Vehicles, 76
DeVille, Pam, 71, 76, 100, 115, 125, 151
Disaster Recovery Center, 42
Domingue Recreation Center, 134
Durel, Joey, 19, 38, 51-52, 76, 84, 149-51

Ellis, Teresa, 38

Ellison, Guy, 87-88

Family Net, 98, 123-24
Federal Emergency Management Agency (FEMA), 17-18, 21, 40-43, 51-52, 76, 79-80, 87-88, 92-93, 96, 106, 116, 118, 123, 125-27, 133, 142-43, 152
fire marshal, 111
Foundation for Hope, 49-50, 85, 96, 124-25, 139
Fowler, Captain, 22
funding, 93

Gage, Faye, 108
George, Felicia, 107
Girard Park, 56
Goodwill, 57
Goodwyn, David, 79
Grand Isle, 17
Greater New Orleans Writing Project, 107
Grief Center, 56
Guidry, Don, 77

Haspel, Jane, 107
Hawthorne, Dan, 88
Health and Human Services, 44
hyper cleaning, 77

Information Desk, 87-88

Jennings, Karen, 19
Judice, Kip, 32-33, 84-87, 132

Kids' Play Day, 56

Lafayette, 20-22, 93

Lafayette Coming Together (LCT), 78-80
Lafayette Consolidated Government, 20, 22, 50, 52
Lafayette General Hospital, 82
Lafayette in a New Century (LINC) plan, 149
Lafayette Parish Schools, 20, 90-91
Lafayette Police Department, 22
Landry, Patrick, 91
Langlinais, Ashton, 36, 78
Laroussini, Jill, 92
LeBreton, Guy, 64
Leonard, Audrey, 61, 135
Live Oak Writing Project, 107
Louisiana Association for the Education of Homeless Children and Youth, 60, 90, 104
Louisiana State Police, 70
Louth, Richard, 108

McGonegal, Tish, 59, 108
Marlink, Jayne, 105
Master's Commission, 22
Mayers, Edye, 115
Melancon, Denise, 90
Mills, Gene, 47
Mississippi River, 17
Mittiga, Jody, 45
Moorman, Linette, 107
Morial Convention Center, New Orleans, 71
Movassaghi, Kam, 150

Nagin, Ray, 21, 127, 133

National Guard, 33, 40, 51, 78, 83-84, 86-87, 101-2, 126, 128
National Writing Project, 58-59
Neiss, Sherry Red Owl, 108
New Orleans housing developments, 72
New Orleans Police Department, 84
New Vox Communications, 36
New York City Writing Project, 107
Northside High School, 84

Office of Emergency Preparedness, 31, 52
Our Lady of Lourdes Hospital, 37, 77
Owen, Lisa, 82

Parkerson Brinckerhoff, 42
Pastor's Resource Council (PRC), 47-50, 96, 127
Penrod, Diane, 104
Peterson, Nancy, 59
Philadelphia Writing Project, 108
Prado, Dave, 36
Proctor, James, 23, 89
Public Works Department, 20, 51

Reeves, Joanne, 141
Rhode Island Writing Project, 108
Roemer, Marjorie, 108

St. Julien, John, 79-80, 118
St. Julien, Layne, 79

Salvation Army, 60, 116
Sandlin, Leslie, 88
Schaefer, Tricia, 42, 87, 125-27, 133
Secangu Writing and Action Project, 108
Sheehan, John Francis, Jr., 18, 40, 42-44
Siebert, Hotie, 123-24
Single Source Supply, 48
Smith, Nate, 96
Social Security, 19, 88
Southern University, Shreveport, 114
Stanley, Dee, 52-53
Steegler, Carrie, 50
Superdome, 87

Texas Children's Hospital, 70
Thomas, DeMarcus, 19, 82
Trahan, Lee, 46
Transitional Academic Program for Students (TAPS), 90-92, 98

Tulane University Hospital, 70
Tyrrell, Mark, 35, 81-82

UCI Communications, 36, 78
University Medical Center, Lafayette, 46, 68-69, 78
University of Louisiana at Lafayette (ULL), 91-92, 100, 117, 151-52

Vermilion Bay, 17
Voisin, Sam, 18, 34

White, Celeste, 87-88
White, Elaine, 107
WOW Technologies, 36, 78
Wright, Michelle, 67-71, 89, 135-36
Wright, Pat, 106, 117
Wyatt, Charles, 45

Zeringue, Chad, 91
Zydetec, 80